Eliza A Pitkin, Julia A Pye

Invalid Cookery

A manual of recipes for the preparation of food for the sick and convalescent: to which is added a chapter of practical suggestions for the sickroom

Eliza A Pitkin, Julia A Pye

Invalid Cookery

A manual of recipes for the preparation of food for the sick and convalescent: to which is added a chapter of practical suggestions for the sickroom

ISBN/EAN: 9783744785211

Printed in Europe, USA, Canada, Australia, Japan

Cover: Foto ©Lupo / pixelio.de

More available books at **www.hansebooks.com**

INVALID COOKERY:

A MANUAL

OF

RECIPES FOR THE PREPARATION OF FOOD

FOR THE

SICK AND CONVALESCENT;

TO WHICH IS ADDED

A CHAPTER OF PRACTICAL SUGGESTIONS FOR THE SICK-ROOM,

BY MRS. JULIA A. PYE.

EDITED BY

MRS. ELIZA A. PITKIN.

CHICAGO:
1880.

PREFACE.

This work has been compiled with a desire to contribute as far as possible to the comfort and pleasure of suffering invalids, and to aid those on whom devolves the sacred obligation of ministering to their wants.

The preparation of nourishing food for the sick is an art in which few persons are skilled, and it has been the endeavor of the author to supply a long-felt necessity by giving a varied assortment of *tested* recipes for plain, digestible, nutritious diet, all of which have been submitted to, and approved by, physicians of high authority, to whom I am indebted for books, valuable advice, and encouragement.

Great care has been taken to make it of practical value to the most inexperienced in culinary matters.

THE AUTHOR.

CONTENTS.

BEEF TEAS—
  No. 1 15
  No. 2 15
  with Oatmeal or Rice......... 16
  Raw 16
BEEF SANDWICH............. 113
BLANC MANGE—
  Arrowroot 94
  Corn Starch 96
  Farina 95
  Irish Moss................. 94
  Rennet 93
  Rice Cream................ 95
BREADS—
  Wheat 40
  Beef Tea.................. 41
  Graham 42
  Beef Tea Crackers 43
  Graham Gems 44
  Graham Wafers 43
  Hoe Cake 44
  Muffins 45
  Oatmeal Cakes 44
  Rusk 113
  Toast, Cracker............. 47
  Toast, Cream. 47
  Toast, Dry 46

Toast, Pilot 48
Toast, Water............... 46
Unleavened Wafers 46
BROILS—
  Beef Steak 31
  Birds 35
  Chicken................... 33
  Fish 36
  Mutton 32
  Oysters 36
  Quail 34
  Scraped Beef Steak 32
  Squabs.................... 35
  Squirrels 35
  Sweetbreads................ 32
  Tripe 33
  Venison 34
BROTHS—
  Beef...................... 17
  Chicken 18
  Egg 112
  Mutton 17
  Oyster 18
CAKES—
  Plain Sponge...............111
  White Sponge 110

CONTENTS.

CAUDLES —
  Egg 91
  Orange 92
  Rice 91

CREAMS —
  Bavarian Golden 108
  Bavarian White 107
  Ice No. 1 109
  Ice No. 2 109
  Tapioca 106

CUSTARDS —
  Baked 88
  Boiled 89
  Rennet 87
  Sago No. 1 89
  Sago No. 2 90

DRINKS —
  Broma 60
  Cocoa 59
  Chocolate 59
  Coffee 55
    Barley No. 1 57
    Barley No. 2 57
    and Egg 56
    Rice 57
  Milk and Water 112
  Sago Milk 77
  Tea 58
    Bran 58
    Milk 59
  Currant Shrub 72
  Grog 74
  Rennet Wine 74

Sherry Claret or Catawba Cobbler 74
  Toddy 73
  Koumiss No. 1 78
  Koumiss No. 2 79
  Mint Julep 73
  Porteree 75
  Syllabub 75
  Toast Wine 75
  Horsford's Acid Phosphates ... 72
  Mulled Wine 77
  Mulled Cider 78
  Orgeat 76

EGGS —
  Caudled 39
  Omelet 39
  Poached, on Toast 38

EGG NOGGS —
  Egg Nogg 81
    Hot 82
    Summer 82
  Egg and Brandy 84
  Egg Flip 84
  Egg and Wine No. 1 ... 83
  Egg and Wine No. 2 ... 84

ESSENCES —
  Beef Essence No. 1 ... 11
  Beef Essence No. 2 ... 11
  Beef Essence No. 3 ... 12
  Beef Essence, in Haste ... 12
  Beef Essence, Jellied ... 13
  Beef Juice 13
  Beef Juice and Ice Cream ... 14
  Oyster Essence 14

CONTENTS.

FLUMMERIES—
  Bran 85
  Oatmeal No. 1 85
  Oatmeal No. 2 86

GRUELS—
  Cornmeal 53
  Farina 54
  Oatmeal 53
  Rice 54
  Rice Flour 55

INFANTS' FOOD—
  Almond Milk 116
  Arrowroot 116
  Barley 114
  Bran 115
  Milk 114
  Oatmeal 115
  Boiled Flour 117

JELLIES—
  Arrowroot 100
  Barley 101
  Calf's Foot 103
  Chicken 99
  Corn Starch Wine 100
  Gelatine Wine 104

LEMONADES—
  Egg 71
  Flax Seed 71
  Irish Moss 71
  No. 1 70
  No. 2 70

NUTRITIVE ENEMATA 118

PANADAS—
  Cracker 50
  Chicken 49
  Hard Cider 50
  Toast 51

PAPS—
  Arrowroot 51
  Corn Starch 52
  Rice Flour 52

PRACTICAL SUGGESTIONS FOR
  THE SICK-ROOM 121

PUDDINGS—
  Bread 97
  Rice 97
  Steamed Rice 98
  Browned Rice 98

PUNCHES—
  Egg and Milk 81
  Milk 80
  80
  76
  81
  93

  Rennet Curd 93
  Beef Soup in Haste 21   Haste 21
  Brown Flour Soup 24   24
  are by error indexed under head of
  PUNCHES.

CONTENTS.

SOUPS—
  Chicken 23
  Macaroni 19
  Mutton 22
  Oyster 23
  Potato 24
  Rice 20
  Sago 20
  Stock for Soup 19
  Tapioca 21
  Toast 21

STEWS—
  Birds 29
  Chicken 27
  Lamb 25
  Oysters 30
  Squirrel 28
  Sweetbreads 26
  Tripe 26
  Venison 28

VEGETABLES—
  Asparagus 37
  Celery 37
  Potato 37
  Spinach 38

WATERS—
  Almond Barley 61
  Apple No. 1 66
  Apple No. 2 67
  Barley 61
  Bran 60
  Burnt Toast 64
  Egg 62
  Gum Arabic 65
  Jelly 67
  Jelly, Hot 67
  Mint 65
  Oatmeal No. 1 62
  Oatmeal No. 2 63
  Peach 66
  Rice 63
  Tamarind 66
  Tapioca 64
  Toast 64

WHEYS—
  Lemon 69
  Rennet 68
  Tamarind 69
  Vinegar 69
  Wine 68

INVALID COOKERY.

ESSENCES.

BEEF ESSENCE NO. 1.

One pound of lean, juicy beef.
Half a saltspoonful of salt.

Mince the meat, put it into a wide-mouthed bottle or fruit-jar, cover tight, and set it in a kettle of cold water over a slow fire; boil three hours.

Stir well, strain, and add the salt; when cold, remove every particle of fat.

Time required, about three hours.

N. B.—In rewarming beef essence or tea, never heat it beyond the point at which it is required for use.

BEEF ESSENCE NO. 2.

One pound of lean, juicy beef.
Half a saltspoonful of salt.

Mince the meat, put it into an earthen jar with a tight cover, place the jar in a moderately hot oven and let it remain three hours.

Stir it well, strain through a sieve, and add the salt; when cold, remove all the fat.
Time required, three hours.

BEEF ESSENCE NO. 3.

One pound of lean, juicy beef.
Half a pint of cold water.
Half a saltspoonful of salt.

Remove every particle of fat and skin from the steak, and pound it well with a mallet.

Fold the meat twice, put it on a broiler over a very hot fire and let it broil two minutes.

Mince it fine, put it into a wide-mouthed bottle or fruit-jar with the water, and let it soak two hours.

Then cover close, and set the jar in a kettle of cold water over a slow fire.

Boil slowly and steadily, twelve hours.

Stir well, strain, and add the salt to the essence.
Time required, twelve hours.

BEEF ESSENCE IN HASTE.

One pound of steak, cut from the top of the round.
Half a saltspoonful of salt.

Remove every particle of fat and skin from the steak, and mince the meat fine.

Put it into a dry stew-pan over a slow fire, and let

the juice ooze from it about six minutes, stirring all the time to prevent sticking.

Strain, add the salt, and serve either hot or ice-cold.

Time required, about six minutes.

BEEF ESSENCE—JELLIED.

One tablespoonful of gelatine.
Two tablespoonfuls of cold water.
One-fourth of a pint of beef essence.

Dissolve the gelatine in the water by slowly heating it, and stirring at the same time.

Warm the essence, stir it into the gelatine, and turn it into a cup to cool and harden.

Serve very cold.

Time required, about three hours.

N. B.—The patient sometimes tires of *drinking* beef essence or tea, and this may be an agreeable change.

BEEF JUICE.

One pound of lean, juicy beef.
Half a saltspoonful of salt.

Place the meat on a broiler over a clear hot fire, and broil until it is heated through.

Squeeze the juice into a hot cup, and add the salt.

Serve hot with toast or crackers.

Time required, about twenty minutes.

BEEF JUICE AND ICE CREAM.

Four tablespoonfuls of beef juice without salt.
Four tablespoonfuls of rich, sweet cream.
Four teaspoonfuls of sugar.
Four drops of essence of vanilla.

Put all the ingredients into a freezer, and stir until the sugar is dissolved.

Freeze in the same manner as you would any other ice cream.

Time required, about an hour.

N. B.—This is both palatable and nutritious.

OYSTER ESSENCE.

Half a pint of oysters.
One saltspoonful of salt.

Wash and drain the oysters, cut them into small pieces, and put them into a stew-pan over a slow fire.

Simmer until all the juice is extracted, then strain. Add the salt, and serve hot, with toasted crackers.

Time required, about ten minutes.

BEEF TEAS.

BEEF TEA NO. 1.

One pound of lean, juicy beef.
Half a pint of cold water.
One saltspoonful of salt.

Mince the meat, put it into a stew-pan with the water and salt, and soak one hour.

Cover closely, and simmer *very gently* ten or twelve minutes; stir well, strain, and set aside to cool; when cold, remove all the fat.

This should be kept in a very cold place, and heated only in quantities required for immediate use.

Time required after soaking, ten or twelve minutes.

N. B.—If required in haste, the soaking may be omitted.

BEEF TEA NO. 2.

One pound of lean, juicy beef.
One saltspoonful of salt.
Half a pint of warm water.

Broil the meat over a clear, hot fire, until it is heated through.

Then put it into a bowl, sprinkle the salt over it, and add the water; cover closely, and keep hot (but do not boil) one hour.

Strain, and serve hot, with toast or unleavened wafers.

Time required, about one hour.

RAW BEEF TEA.

One pound of lean steak, from the top of the round.
Half a saltspoonful of salt.
Half a pint of cold water.

Mince the meat, put it into a bowl with the salt and water, and let it soak two hours.

Squeeze through a meat or lemon squeezer, and drink the juice ice cold.

Time required, about two hours.

N. B.—This should be served in a claret-colored glass, as the sight of blood will sometimes nauseate the patient.

BEEF TEA, WITH OATMEAL OR RICE.

One pint of beef tea No. 1.
Two tablespoonfuls of cooked oatmeal or rice.
Four tablespoonfuls of boiling water.

Put the beef tea into a saucepan, and heat to the boiling point.

Blend the oatmeal with the boiling water, and stir it into the beef tea.

Add a little salt, and a shake of black pepper if desired.

Serve hot, with toast, crackers, or unleavened wafers.

Time required, ten or fifteen minutes.

BROTHS.

BEEF BROTH.

One pound of lean, juicy beef.
One pint of cold water.
Half a teaspoonful of salt.

Mince the meat, put it into a stew-pan with the water and salt, and boil slowly one hour.

Strain, add a shake of black pepper, if allowed, and serve hot, with strips of dry toast.

Time required, one hour.

MUTTON BROTH.

Two pounds of lean, juicy mutton.
One quart of cold water.
One teaspoonful of salt.

Remove every particle of fat and skin from the meat; then cut it up, put it into a stew-pan with the water and salt, and boil slowly an hour and a half.

Strain, and set it away to cool; when cold, remove all fat and dregs, and heat the broth as required.

Time required, two hours.

CHICKEN BROTH.

Three pounds of tender chicken.
Two quarts of cold water.
Two scant teaspoonfuls of salt.

Skin the chicken (if it is very fat), cut it up, and pound the pieces with a mallet until the bones are broken.

Put it into a stew-pan with the water and salt, and boil slowly two hours; strain, and set aside to cool.

When cold, remove all fat and dregs, and heat as required for use.

Time required, two hours.

OYSTER BROTH.

One pint of oysters.
Half a pint of cold water.
Half a teaspoonful of salt.
A shake of black pepper.

Cut the oysters into small pieces, put them into a stew-pan with the water and salt, and simmer slowly ten minutes.

Skim, strain, and add the pepper.

Serve hot, with toasted crackers.

Time required, about fifteen minutes.

SOUPS.

STOCK FOR SOUP.

Two pounds of the shin of beef.
Two pounds of round or shoulder steak.
Two quarts of cold water.
Two teaspoonfuls of salt.

Wash the meat, put it into a soup-kettle with the cold water and salt, bring slowly to a boil, and skim.

Then let it simmer until the meat is ready to drop to pieces, strain, and set the stock aside to cool; when cold, remove all fat and dregs.

This should be kept in a cold place, but not where it will freeze, and used, when required, for the foundation of soups.

Time required for cooking, about six hours.

MACARONI SOUP.

Half a stick of macaroni.
One-fourth of a pint of cold water.
One pint of boiling stock.
A light shake of black pepper.

Soak the macaroni in the water ten minutes, and simmer in the same thirty minutes.

Then cut it into small pieces and drop them into the boiling stock.

Add the pepper, stew gently ten minutes, and serve hot

Time required, almost an hour.

RICE SOUP.

Two tablespoonfuls of boiled rice.
One pint of boiling stock.
The yolk of half an egg, well beaten.
Four tablespoonfuls of sweet cream.

Rub the rice through a wire sieve into the boiling stock, simmer two minutes, and remove from the fire.

Beat the egg and cream together, and pour it into the stock, stirring all the while to prevent curdling.

Heat to the boiling-point, add a shake of pepper if desired, and serve immediately.

Time required six or eight minutes.

SAGO SOUP.

Half a tablespoonful of pearl sago.
Three tablespoonfuls of cold water.
One pint of boiling stock.
A light shake of pepper.

After the sago has been well washed and drained, soak it in the cold water four or five hours.

Then put it into the stock, simmer until clear, add the pepper, and serve with toasted crackers.

Time required after soaking, half an hour.

TAPIOCA SOUP.

One teaspoonful of tapioca.
One-fourth of a pint of warm water.
Half a pint of stock.

Soak the tapioca in the water over night, then simmer it in the same water until smooth and clear; add the stock, and cook three minutes longer.

If required, more salt may be added, and, if allowed, a slight shake of black pepper.

Time required after soaking, about half an hour.

TOAST SOUP.

Two tablespoonfuls of toast crumbs.
One-fourth of a pint of boiling water.
Half a pint of boiling stock.
A shake of pepper.

Soak the crumbs in the boiling water two minutes, add the stock, and simmer slowly eight minutes.

Season with a light shake of pepper, and serve hot, with dry toast or crackers.

Time required, ten minutes.

BEEF SOUP IN HASTE.

One pound of lean steak.
One pint of cold water.
Half a teaspoonful of salt.

A piece of celery two inches long (if desired).
Two tablespoonfuls of cooked rice.
One tablespoonful of toast crumbs.
A shake of black pepper.

Mince the meat, put it into a stew-pan with the water, salt and celery, and boil slowly thirty minutes.

Add the rice and toast crumbs, and boil fifteen minutes longer.

Take the meat and celery out, pour the soup into a bowl, and shake a very little pepper over the top.

Serve hot, with crackers or toast.

Time required, about three-quarters of an hour.

MUTTON SOUP.

One pound of lean, juicy mutton.
One quart of cold water.
One teaspoonful of salt.
One tablespoonful of uncooked rice.
One teaspoonful of chopped parsley.
A shake of black pepper.

Remove every particle of fat and skin from the meat, put it into a stew-pan with the water and salt, boil thirty minutes, and skim.

Add the rice, parsley and pepper, and boil slowly one hour and a half.

Remove the meat and serve the soup very hot, with toast or crackers.

Time required, two hours.

CHICKEN SOUP.

One pint of chicken broth.
Two tablespoonfuls of cooked rice.
One-fourth of a teaspoonful of chopped parsley.
A light shake of black pepper.

Put all the ingredients into a stew-pan and simmer together twenty minutes.

Serve hot, with dry toast or unleavened wafers.

Time required, about twenty minutes.

OYSTER SOUP.

One pint of oysters.
Half a pint of cold water.
Half a teaspoonful of salt.
One teaspoonful of butter.
One teaspoonful of cracker flour.
Three tablespoonfuls of cream.
A shake of black pepper.
Six fine, whole oysters.

Cut the pint of oysters into small pieces, put them into a stew-pan with the water and salt, and simmer ten or fifteen minutes; skim well and strain.

Rub the butter and cracker flour to a smooth paste; blend enough of the broth with it to make it the consistency of cream, and pour it into the boiling broth.

Add the cream, pepper, and whole oysters.

Boil up once, and serve hot, with crackers.

Time required, about twenty minutes.

POTATO SOUP.

One medium sized potato.
One pint of boiling water.
One saltspoonful of salt.
Two tablespoonfuls of rich cream.
A shake of black pepper.

Pare, and chop the potato fine, put it into a stewpan with the water and salt, and boil until thoroughly done.

Add the cream and pepper, simmer three minutes longer, and serve hot, with dry toast or unleavened wafers.

Time required, about half an hour.
N. B.—This soup is not good warmed over.

BROWNED FLOUR SOUP.

One tablespoonful of browned flour.
One teaspoonful of butter.
Half a saltspoonful of salt.
Two tablespoonfuls of warm water.
Half a pint of boiling water.
One slice of dry toast.

Rub the flour, butter and salt to a smooth paste, and blend it with the warm water.

Pour it slowly into the boiling water, stirring all the while to prevent lumps.

Cut the toast into small squares, put them into a bowl and pour the soup over them.
Time required, about thirty minutes.
N. B.—This soup is recommended in cases of bowel or summer complaints.

STEWS.

STEWED LAMB.

One pound of loin chops.
One pint of hot water.
Half a teaspoonful of salt.
One teaspoonful of flour.
Three tablespoonfuls of cold water.

After the skin and all unnecessary fat have been removed from the chops, put them into a stew-pan with the hot water and salt; boil up quickly and skim.

Cover close, and simmer until the meat is tender, but not so that it will drop from the bones.

Blend the flour and cold water together, stir it into the stew, and boil one minute to cook the flour.

If not salt enough, add a little more, and, if allowed, a shake of black pepper.

Serve *very hot*, in a hot dish.
Time required, two hours.

STEWED TRIPE.

Half a pound of *fresh* honey-comb tripe.
Half a pint of milk.
Half a teaspoonful of salt.
A shake of black pepper.
One teaspoonful of butter.
One scant teaspoonful of flour.
Three tablespoonfuls of sweet cream.

Cut the tripe into short, narrow strips, put them into a stew-pan with the milk, salt, butter and pepper, and simmer until the milk is reduced *to* one-third.

Blend the flour and cream well together, and stir it into the stew; simmer two minutes longer, and serve in a hot, covered dish.

Time required, about half an hour.
N. B.—This is a very digestible and palatable dish.

STEWED SWEETBREADS.

One fine, large pair of sweetbreads.
One scant teaspoonful of salt.
One teaspoonful of flour.
One teaspoonful of butter.
One-fourth of a pint of cream.
Half a teaspoonful of chopped parsley.
A light shake of black pepper.

Remove every particle of skin and fat from the

sweetbreads, wash thoroughly, and let them lie in cold water one hour to whiten.

Then put them into a stew-pan, with enough boiling water to cover; throw in a teaspoonful of salt, and boil briskly thirty minutes, or until done through.

Pour off the boiling water, cover with cold, and let them stand ten or fifteen minutes.

When cold and firm, cut into small, square pieces, and sprinkle over the salt and flour.

Put them into a clean stew-pan with the butter, cream, parsley and pepper, and simmer ten minutes.

Serve in a hot, covered dish.

Time required, about two hours.

STEWED CHICKEN.

One chicken.
One quart of hot water, not boiling.
One teaspoonful of salt.
Four tablespoonfuls of cold water.
Two teaspoonfuls of flour.
Half a saltspoonful of pepper.

Select a young, tender, fat chicken, weighing about two pounds; clean thoroughly, "cut it up," and let it lie in cold water one hour.

Then put it into a stew-pan, with the hot water and salt, cover close, and stew gently until the meat is almost tender enough to drop from the bones.

Blend the cold water, flour and pepper together,

and stir it into the stew while boiling; simmer one minute longer to cook the flour.

Time required, about two hours.

STEWED VENISON.

Two pounds of loin chops.
One quart of hot water.
One scant teaspoonful of salt.
Two teaspoonfuls of flour.
Two teaspoonfuls of butter.
One teaspoonful of port wine.

Remove *all* the fat and skin from the chops, put them into a stew-pan with the water and salt, and simmer until the meat is tender, but not so that it will drop from the bones.

Melt the butter in a frying-pan, stir the flour into it, and heat slowly until it is a delicate brown; blend enough of the gravy with it to make it about the consistency of cream, and stir it into the stew while boiling.

Add the wine, simmer two minutes, and serve hot, with currant jelly.

Time required, about two hours.

STEWED SQUIRREL.

A pair of young, tender squirrels.
One pint of hot water.

One even teaspoonful of salt.
Two teaspoonfuls of butter.
One teaspoonful of flour.
One teaspoonful of sherry wine.
One-fourth of a saltspoonful of black pepper.

Skin, clean and quarter the squirrels, and let them soak in cold water one hour.

Then put them into a stew-pan with the hot water and salt, bring quickly to a boil, and skim; cover close, and simmer until the meat is tender.

Melt the butter, stir the flour into it, and heat slowly till it is a delicate brown; blend enough of the gravy with it to make it about the consistency of cream, and stir it into the stew while boiling; simmer two minutes longer.

Add the wine and pepper, and serve in a hot, covered dish.

Time required, about two hours.

STEWED BIRDS.

Twelve small birds.
One pint of hot water.
One even teaspoonful of salt.
Two teaspoonfuls of butter.
One teaspoonful of flour.
A shake of pepper if desired.

After the birds have been carefully cleaned, put them into a porcelain-lined stew-pan with the water and salt; cover close, and simmer until the meat is almost tender enough to drop from the bones and the water is reduced to one-third.

Rub the butter and flour to a smooth paste; add enough of the gravy to it to make it about the consistency of cream, and stir it into the stew while boiling; simmer one minute longer to cook the flour; add the pepper, and serve in a hot, covered dish.

Time required, from a half to three quarters of an hour.

N. B.—Plover, reed-birds and snipe are delicious cooked in this way.

STEWED OYSTERS.

Half a pint of large, fat oysters.
One-fourth of a pint of cold water.
Half a teaspoonful of salt.
One teaspoonful of butter.
One teaspoonful of cracker-flour.
A tablespoonful of cream.
A shake of black pepper.

Put the oysters into a bowl, and pour the water over them; then, with a silver fork, lift each one out and put it into another dish.

Strain the liquor through a fine sieve, then boil, and skim.

Rub the salt, butter and cracker-flour to a smooth paste; blend enough of the broth with it to make it about tne consistency of cream, and pour it into the boiling broth.

Simmer one minute; add the cream, pepper and oysters, and boil up once.

Serve immediately, with oyster crackers.

Time required, about ten minutes.

BROILS.

BROILED BEEFSTEAK.

Select a tender, juicy piece of beef, about an inch thick (a cut from the tenderloin if possible), also a cut of the same size from the round.

Place both on a heated broiler over a bright, clear fire (of charcoal if convenient), and as soon as the steak is seared on one side, turn and sear the other to prevent the escape of juice. Turn several times while cooking, and when sufficiently done, remove the tenderloin from the broiler to a hot plate and season with salt, butter and pepper.

Sprinkle a little salt over the other piece of steak, and with a meat or lemon squeezer press all the juice from it over the tenderloin.

Cover with a hot plate and serve immediately.

Time required, six or seven minutes.

SCRAPED BEEFSTEAK.

Scrape three or four tablespoonfuls of raw beef from a tender, juicy piece, and with a knife press it into an oval cake about three-quarters of an inch thick.

Rub a little warm (not melted) butter over it and lay it on a *very hot* frying-pan; when sufficiently cooked on both sides, season daintily with butter, pepper and salt.

Serve between hot plates.

Time required for cooking, about three minutes.

BROILED MUTTON CHOP.

Remove all skin and fat from a loin chop about three-quarters of an inch thick.

Place it on a heated broiler over a bright, clear fire, and turn it frequently while cooking.

When sufficiently done on both sides, remove it from the broiler to a hot plate, and season with salt, and, if allowed, a little butter and pepper.

Serve between hot plates.

Time required, about six minutes.

BROILED SWEETBREADS.

Select a fine, large pair of sweetbreads, remove *every particle* of *skin* and *fat* from them, and let them lie in cold water one hour to whiten.

Then put them into a stew-pan with enough boiling water to cover, throw in a teaspoonful of salt, and boil briskly thirty minutes or until done through.

Pour off the boiling water, cover with cold, and let them stand ten or fifteen minutes.

Wipe dry, split lengthwise, and rub a little warm butter all over them.

Broil over bright coals till a delicate brown on both sides; season sparingly with butter and pepper, and more salt if required.

Serve between hot plates.

Time required, about two hours.

BROILED TRIPE.

Choose the thick, honey-comb tripe, either fresh or pickled; wipe it dry, rub a very little melted butter over it, dredge well with cracker-flour, and broil over a brisk fire until slightly browned on both sides.

Season lightly with butter, pepper and salt, and serve between hot plates.

Time required, about seven minutes.

N. B.—This is light and nutritious.

BROILED SPRING CHICKEN.

Select a young, tender, fat chicken. After it has been thoroughly cleaned and allowed to cool, split it at the back and break the breast-bone down with a mallet.

Put it on a heated broiler over a clear (but not too hot) fire, and turn frequently while cooking.

When about half done, season with salt, and a little butter and pepper; broil again till well done, but not dry.

Serve between hot plates.

Time required for cooking, about half an hour.

BROILED VENISON STEAK.

Select a tender cut of venison, about an inch thick.

Broil over a clear, hot fire until cooked through, but not dry.

Season with butter, salt and pepper, with a few bits of currant jelly placed about the top of it.

Serve between hot plates.

Time required, seven or eight minutes.

BROILED QUAIL.

After the bird has been thoroughly cleaned, washed, and wiped dry, split it at the back, and break down the breast-bone with a mallet.

Rub warm (not melted) butter over it, and broil over a clear fire, turning frequently while cooking.

When done, season with butter, pepper and salt.

Serve on thin, slightly buttered toast.

Time required, about twenty minutes.

BROILED SQUABS.

When the squabs (young pigeons) are about one month old, they are in their prime for broiling, and are considered a very delicate dish.

They should be prepared and broiled the same as quail.

Time required, about twenty minutes.

BROILED BIRDS.

When preparing small birds for broiling, never skin them, or even break the skin if it can be avoided.

After they have been carefully cleaned, and wiped dry, rub a little warm butter over each, and broil them over a bright, but not too brisk, fire, turning frequently while cooking.

Season with butter, pepper and salt.

Serve on thin slices of slightly buttered toast.

Time required, ten or fifteen minutes.

Plover, reed-birds and snipe are especially tempting to the palate of the invalid.

BROILED SQUIRREL.

Select a young, tender squirrel; in cleaning it, great care should be taken to prevent any of the fur from remaining on the meat.

When thoroughly cleaned, and wiped dry, broil in the same manner as quail.

Time required for a young squirrel, about twenty minutes.

BROILED FISH.

After the fish has been thoroughly cleaned, washed, and wiped dry, split, and lay it in a folding boiler over a clear, bright fire.

Turn frequently while cooking.

When well done (not dry), and a delicate brown on both sides, season sparingly with butter, salt and pepper.

Serve between hot plates.

Time required, about twenty minutes for a two-pound fish.

N. B.—Broiling is the best mode of cooking brook trout, whitefish or shad.

Do not attempt to broil a fish unless it is *perfectly fresh.*

BROILED OYSTERS.

Select large, fat oysters, wash, and wipe dry.

Place them in the folds of a clean towel, and pat gently with the hands to plump them.

Season with salt and a little pepper.

Heat and butter the wires of a folding broiler,—one with the wires close together,— and place the oysters in it over a *very* hot fire.

Broil quickly, and, when *just cooked through*, lay them on slightly buttered and moistened toast, which should be ready before you begin to cook the oysters.

Serve between hot plates.

Time required for broiling, two or three minutes.

VEGETABLES.

BAKED POTATOES.

Wash, and wipe dry, as many potatoes as required, being careful to have them of uniform size.

Bake in a brisk oven until they will yield to pressure between the fingers; remove at once from the oven and break the skin to let out the steam.

Serve immediately, with salt, and, if allowed, butter and pepper.

Time required, from thirty to forty minutes.

STEWED CELERY.

After the celery has been thoroughly washed, cut the stalks into pieces four or five inches long, lay them (all one way) in a saucepan, with just enough slightly salted boiling water to cover.

Boil slowly until tender; then drain, and season with a little butter and pepper.

Time required, about an hour.

ASPARAGUS.

Bind the asparagus into a bundle with a piece of tape, keeping the buds one way; cut the stalks of equal length, and be careful to cut off all that is tough. Put it into a porcelain-lined kettle, with enough slightly salted, boiling water to cover, and boil until tender.

Season delicately with butter and pepper, and more salt if desired.

Time required, about half an hour.

SPINACH.

Select young, tender spinach, pick it over carefully, and wash thoroughly in cold water.

Then put it into a *porcelain* kettle, sprinkle over a little salt, and simmer twenty minutes, or until the spinach is tender.

Strain through a colander, cut fine, and season daintily with butter and pepper, a few drops of lemon juice, and more salt if required.

Time required, about half an hour.

N. B.—When the spinach is washed, sufficient water adheres to it to cook it.

EGGS.

POACHED EGGS ON TOAST.

One quart of boiling water.
One teaspoonful of salt.
Two eggs.
A shake of black pepper.

Put the water and salt into a well-greased frying-pan, break the eggs into a saucer, and slip them carefully into the water while boiling.

Do not boil again, but allow the eggs to remain in the water until the white is set and the yolk as much cooked as is desired.

Take them out carefully, so as not to break the yolks, lay them on thin slices of slightly buttered toast, and shake a very little black pepper over them.

Time required, about six minutes.

CAUDLED EGGS.

Put the eggs into a saucepan of boiling water, allowing a pint for each egg, cover close, and set it on the back part of the stove (where it will keep hot, but not boil), and let it remain six or seven minutes.

Have a hot glass or cup ready, and empty the egg from the shell into it as quickly as possible.

Season with salt, and a little butter and pepper if allowed.

Serve immediately.

Time required, seven or eight minutes.

OMELET.

The yolk of one egg.
One tablespoonful of sweet milk.
One-third of a teaspoonful of corn-starch.
Half a saltspoonful of salt.
A light shake of pepper.
The whites of two eggs.

Beat the yolk of the egg until it is light, add the milk, corn-starch, salt and pepper, and stir until all are well blended.

Beat the whites of the two eggs to a *stiff*, *dry froth*, and stir it lightly into the yellow.

Heat a frying-pan (about the size of a small tea plate), grease it lightly with butter, and pour the omelet mixture into it; cook slowly until it is "set," then cut across with a knife, fold, and serve *immediately*.

Time required, about six minutes.

BREADS.

BREAD.

Six quarts of sifted flour.
One pint of bran water.*
One quart of scalding milk.
Two teaspoonfuls of salt.
One pint of mashed potato.
A piece of compressed yeast an inch and a half square.
Three tablespoonfuls of warm water.

Put five quarts of the flour into a bread-bowl or tray, make a hollow in the center and pour the bran

* See Bran-water.

water and milk into it; add the salt, potato, and yeast which has been dissolved in the warm water.

Stir vigorously with a wooden spoon till well mixed, then add the remainder of the flour, and when that is well worked in, put it on the breadboard and knead twenty minutes, using only enough *extra* flour to keep from sticking.

Mould into four loaves, rub a little melted lard over each, and put them into buttered pans, which they should only half fill; set them in a warm place to rise, and when the bread puffs a little over the tops of the pans, place them carefully in the oven and bake until thoroughly done.

Time required, from five to seven hours.

N. B.—Bread made in this way retains more of the wheat flavor than if raised several times.

If kneaded and raised twice, it will be much finer grain; and if three times, will be very light and nice for toast.

BEEF-TEA BREAD.

Two quarts of sifted flour.
Half a pint of bran water.
Half a pint of hot beef tea.
Half a teaspoonful of salt.
A piece of compressed yeast three-quarters of an inch square.
Four tablespoonfuls of cold water.

Put the flour into a bread-bowl, make a hollow in the center and pour the bran water into it.

Add the salt, and yeast which has been dissolved in the cold water; stir with a spoon until well mixed, and knead on the board twenty minutes, using only enough extra flour to keep from sticking.

Mould into two small loaves, rub a little melted lard over each, and put them into buttered pans, which they should only half fill.

Set them in a warm place to rise, and when the bread puffs a little over the tops of the pans, place them carefully in the oven and bake until well done.

Time required, about five hours.

GRAHAM BREAD.

Two quarts of Graham flour.
One quart of white flour.
One quart of warm water.
One-fourth of a pint of home-made yeast.
Six tablespoonfuls of molasses or syrup.
One teaspoonful of salt.

Mix all the ingredients well together and knead five minutes; mould into three loaves, and place each in a well-greased pan that it will only half fill.

Set them in a warm place to rise, and when the bread puffs a little over the tops of the pans, place carefully in the oven and bake one hour.

Time required for raising, about three hours.

BEEF-TEA CRACKERS.

Two tablespoonfuls of butter.
One quart of sifted flour.
Half a pint of beef tea.
Half a teaspoonful of salt.

Rub the butter well into the flour; add the beef tea and salt, and knead half an hour, using only enough extra flour to keep from sticking.

Cut into round cakes with a biscuit-cutter, prick with a fork, and bake in a quick oven to a rich, even brown.

Time required, about one hour.

GRAHAM WAFERS.

One scant quart of Graham flour.
Half a pint of cream.
One teaspoonful of salt.

Mix the ingredients well together, and let the dough stand half an hour.

Roll very thin, cut into small cakes with a biscuit-cutter, and place them on a baking tin that has been dredged with flour.

Prick five or six times with a fork, and bake in a brisk oven.

Time required, nearly an hour.

GRAHAM GEMS.

One quart of Graham flour.
One and a half pints of ice-cold water.

Mix the flour and water together, and stir briskly five minutes.

Pour the batter into very hot, well-greased gem-irons, only half filling them.

Let them remain on the top of the stove one minute, then bake in a *very hot* oven half an hour, or until they are brown.

Time required for mixing and baking, about three-quarters of an hour.

OATMEAL CAKES.

One quart of fine oatmeal.
One pint of warm water.
Four tablespoonfuls of cream.
One scant teaspoonful of salt.

Stir all the ingredients well together, drop with a teaspoon into buttered pans, and bake in a brisk oven.

Time required, about half an hour.

HOE CAKE.

One pint of white cornmeal.
One-fourth of a pint of boiling water.
One saltspoonful of salt.

Stir all the ingredients well together, and let it stand one minute.

Sprinkle a little meal on a hot griddle, and as soon as it browns, mould the dough with the hands into a smooth, round ball; lay it on the griddle, and pat it down until it is about half an inch thick.

Brown quickly on one side (be careful not to burn it), and turn it before the upper side becomes dry; bake slowly until the cake is done through, and brown on both sides.

Time required, about half an hour.

DELICATE MUFFINS.

One egg.
Half a pint of flour.
One saltspoonful of salt.
Half a pint of milk.

Beat the egg (yolk and white together) until very light.

Blend the flour and salt well with the milk, and stir it into the egg.

Pour the batter into *hot*, well-buttered muffin-tins, or (what is better) gem-irons, only half filling them; bake in a quick oven.

Time required for baking, about half an hour.

UNLEAVENED WAFERS.

One quart of sifted flour.
Half a pint of cold water.
One teaspoonful of salt.

Mix the ingredients well together, roll out thin, and cut into small cakes with a biscuit-cutter.

Then roll the cakes as thin as possible, lay them in a pan that has been dredged with flour, and bake in a brisk oven.

Time required, about half an hour.

DRY TOAST.

Toast should be made of very light bread, at least twenty-four hours old.

Cut the bread into slices about three-quarters of an inch thick, and toast slowly over a clear fire — turning frequently, that it may heat through before it begins to brown.

When a delicate brown on both sides, cut the crust edges off, or break them down with the handle of a knife, and butter sparingly.

Serve as hot as possible.

WATER TOAST.

One slice of very light bread, not too fresh.
A piece of butter the size of a chestnut.
Half a saltspoonful of salt.
Five tablespoonfuls of boiling water.

Toast the bread to a rich brown on both sides, and spread the butter evenly over it.

Lay it on a hot plate, sprinkle over the salt, and pour on the boiling water.

Serve between hot plates.

Time required, five or six minutes.

N. B.—A teaspoonful of sugar and a grate of nutmeg over the toast make a pleasant change.

CREAM TOAST.

One slice of very light bread, not too fresh.
Half a saltspoonful of salt.
Four tablespoonfuls of boiling water.
One tablespoonful of *rich* cream.

Toast the bread to a rich brown on both sides, and lay it on a hot plate.

Dissolve the salt in the water, and pour it over the toast.

When it is all soaked up, spread on the cream.

Serve between hot plates.

Time required, about ten minutes.

CRACKER TOAST.

Three water crackers.
One teaspoon even full of butter.
Half a saltspoonful of salt.

Split, and spread the crackers with the butter,

sprinkle over the salt, and pour on as much boiling water as they will absorb.

Then put them carefully on a tin plate, place it on the rack in a brisk oven, and let it remain five minutes.

Serve immediately.

Time required, about half an hour.

PILOT TOAST.

One " pilot biscuit."
One saltspoonful of salt.
Four tablespoonfuls of rich cream.

Split, and cover the biscuit with cold water, and let it stand twenty minutes.

Cover again, place in a moderate oven, and let it remain until the water is all absorbed.

When the biscuit is heated through, and looks "puffy" and light, sprinkle with the salt and pour over the cream.

Serve hot.

Time required, about an hour.

PANADAS.

CHICKEN PANADA.

One full-grown, tender chicken.
Three pints of hot water.
One teaspoonful of salt.
Pepper or nutmeg.

After the chicken has been well cleaned, and allowed to cool, put it (whole) into a kettle with the water and salt, and boil *slowly* until it is well done, but not so that it will drop to pieces.

Take the chicken out of the broth and set both away for three or four hours to cool.

Then remove the skin from the white meat, cut it up, put it into a mortar with two tablespoonfuls of the broth (free from fat), and pound it to a smooth paste.

Add as much broth as will make it thin enough to drink as you would soup.

Boil up once, season with a very little pepper or nutmeg, and strain through a fine sieve.

Serve hot, with toast or unleavened wafers.

Time required, about six hours.

N. B.—Be careful to remove every particle of the fat from the broth before it is added to the paste. If desired richer, stir in two tablespoonfuls of cream; if it is too rich, dilute with boiling water.

HARD CIDER PANADA.

Two slices of nicely browned toast.
One teaspoonful of sugar.
Half a pint of ice-cold water.
One-fourth of a pint of hard cider.

Cut the toast into small squares, and put them into a bowl.

Dissolve the sugar in the water, add the cider to it, and pour the whole over the toast.

Time required, about five minutes.

N. B.—This is very refreshing, especially to a patient who is bilious.

CRACKER PANADA.

Twelve small oyster crackers.
One teaspoon even full of butter.
Two teaspoonfuls of sugar.
One pint of boiling water.
Nutmeg.

Split the crackers, spread each piece with butter, and lay them in a hot bowl.

Sprinkle the sugar over, pour the water on, and grate a very little nutmeg over the top.

Cover the bowl, and let it stand in a hot place four or five minutes.

Time required, about ten minutes.

TOAST PANADA.

One slice of slightly buttered toast.
Two teaspoonfuls of sugar.
Half a saltspoonful of salt.
Two tablespoonfuls of brandy or rum.
Half a pint of boiling water.
Nutmeg.

Cut the toast into small squares, and put them into a hot bowl.

Sprinkle the sugar and salt over, add the brandy, and pour on the boiling water.

Grate a very little nutmeg over the top, and serve immediately.

Time required, ten or fifteen minutes.

PAPS.

ARROWROOT PAP.

One tablespoonful of Bermuda arrowroot.
Four tablespoonfuls of cold milk.
One pint of boiling milk.
One teaspoonful of sugar.
One-fourth of a saltspoonful of cinnamon.
One-fourth of a saltspoonful of salt.

Blend the arrowroot with the cold milk, and pour it slowly into the boiling milk, stirring all the while to prevent lumps and burning.

Simmer ten minutes, and stir in the sugar, cinnamon, and salt.

Time required, about fifteen minutes.

N. B.— A teaspoonful of brandy may be used instead of the cinnamon, or both may be left out if they are not desired.

CORN STARCH PAP.

One tablespoonful of corn starch.
Six tablespoonfuls of cold milk.
One pint of boiling milk.
One teaspoonful of sugar.
One-fourth of a saltspoonful of cinnamon
One-fourth of a saltspoonful of salt.

Blend the starch well with the cold milk, and pour it slowly into the boiling milk, stirring all the while to prevent lumps and burning.

Simmer slowly fifteen minutes, and add the sugar, cinnamon, and salt.

Time required, about twenty minutes.

RICE-FLOUR PAP.

Two teaspoonfuls of rice flour.
Four tablespoonfuls of cold milk.
One pint of boiling milk.
One teaspoonful of sugar.
One-fourth of a saltspoonful of salt.
Half a teaspoonful of brandy.

Blend the flour well with the cold milk, and pour it slowly into the boiling milk, stirring all the while.

Simmer fifteen minutes; add the sugar, salt, and brandy.

Time required, about twenty minutes.

GRUELS.

OATMEAL GRUEL.

One quart of boiling water.
Half a pint of medium oatmeal.
Half a teaspoonful of salt.

Pour the boiling water over the meal, stir it well, and strain through a wire sieve.

Boil the liquid, which is strained off until it thickens and looks clear; if too thick, add boiling water until it is of the desired consistency.

Add the salt, and, if allowed, two tablespoonfuls of sweet cream, which will greatly improve the taste.

Time required, thirty minutes.

CORNMEAL GRUEL.

One tablespoonful of fresh cornmeal.
One quart of boiling water.
One saltspoonful of salt.

Sprinkle the meal into the water while boiling, stirring all the while to prevent lumps.

Add the salt, and simmer slowly two hours; if too thick, thin it with boiling water.

Time required, two hours.

FARINA GRUEL.

One tablespoonful of farina.
One pint of boiling water.
Half a saltspoonful of salt.

Sprinkle the farina into the boiling water, stirring all the time to prevent lumps.

Add the salt, and simmer slowly half an hour.

A tablespoonful of cream will improve the taste of the gruel, and, if allowed, should be stirred in just before it is removed from the fire.

Time required, thirty minutes.

RICE GRUEL.

Two tablespoonfuls of Carolina rice.
Six tablespoonfuls of cold water.
One and a half pints of new milk.
One teaspoonful of sugar.
Half a saltspoonful of salt.

Wash the rice thoroughly, and soak it in the cold water one hour.

Put it into a double kettle with the milk, and simmer until the rice is well done.

Then pulp it through a wire sieve, and add the sugar and salt.

Time required, about two hours.

RICE-FLOUR GRUEL.

Two teaspoonfuls of rice flour.
Four tablespoonfuls of cold water.
Half a pint of boiling water.
One-fourth of a saltspoonful of salt.
One teaspoonful of sugar.
One tablespoonful of cream.

Blend the flour with the cold water, and pour slowly into the boiling water. stirring all the time to prevent lumps and burning.

Simmer ten minutes, then add the salt, sugar, and cream. Drink either hot or cold.

Time required, ten or fifteen minutes.

DRINKS.

COFFEE.

Two tablespoonfuls of freshly ground coffee.
Four tablespoonfuls of cold water.
Half an egg.
One pint of boiling water (freshly boiled).

Put the coffee, cold water, and egg into the coffee-pot, and stir well.

Pour in the boiling water, simmer slowly two minutes, then stir down the grounds.

Let it stand where it will keep very hot (but not boil), five minutes longer.

Strain, and serve hot with cream and sugar; if too strong, dilute with boiling milk or water.

Time required, not over ten minutes.

COFFEE AND EGG.

One large tablespoonful of ground coffee.
One-fourth of an egg.
One-fourth of a pint of boiling water.
One-fourth of a pint of fresh milk.
Four teaspoonfuls of sugar.
One whole egg.
Two tablespoonfuls of *hot* cream.

Put the first four ingredients into a small coffee-pot, and boil five minutes.

Beat the sugar and egg together until stiff and light, and strain the boiling coffee into it, stirring all the while to prevent curdling.

Add the cream, and serve either hot or cold. though it is more palatable when taken hot.

Time required, about ten minutes.

N. B.—This is used when stimulant and nourishment are required, and should only be taken in small quantities. In cases of extreme exhaustion, a stronger decoction of coffee can be used, but only by order of the physician.

BARLEY COFFEE NO. 1.

One pint of browned barley, unground.
Three pints of boiling water.

Put the barley and water into a coffee-pot, and boil slowly half an hour.
Strain, and serve hot, with cream and sugar.
Time required, half an hour.
N. B.—A well beaten egg, stirred through the barley after it is browned, and when about half cold, will clear the coffee when it is made.

BARLEY COFFEE NO. 2.

Half a pint of browned barley, unground.
One quart of fresh, hot milk.

Put the barley and milk into a coffee-pot and simmer fifteen minutes.
Strain, sweeten, and serve hot.
Time required, fifteen minutes.

BROWNED RICE COFFEE.

Six tablespoonfuls of well browned rice.
One pint of boiling water.

Put the rice and water into a coffee-pot and boil twenty minutes.

Strain, and serve hot with cream and sugar.

Time required, about half an hour.

TEA.

Two teaspoonfuls of dry tea.

One pint of boiling water.

Scald a small china or earthenware tea-pot, put in the dry tea and boiling water, cover close, and set it over the steam of the tea-kettle to steep.

Strain, and serve hot with sugar, and cream if desired.

Time required, six or seven minutes.

BRAN TEA.

One pint of good wheat bran.

One quart of boiling water.

Put the bran and water into an earthen tea-pot, set it on the stove where it will *almost* boil, and let it remain there one hour.

Strain, and serve with cream and sugar, just as you would any other tea.

Time required, one hour.

N. B.—This drink is very palatable, and is excellent for both invalids and children.

MILK TEA.

One-fourth of a pint of fresh milk.
One-fourth of a pint of boiling water.
Two teaspoonfuls of cream.
One teaspoonful of sugar.

Put the above ingredients into a cup, and serve as any other tea.

Time required, two minutes.

N. B.—Excellent for children.

CHOCOLATE.

Two tablespoonfuls of scraped chocolate.
Six tablespoonfuls of boiling water.
One pint of boiling milk.
One tablespoonful of cream.
One teaspoonful of sugar.

Dissolve the chocolate in the boiling water and pour it into the boiling milk.

Simmer until it thickens, add the sugar and cream, and serve hot, with toast.

Time required, ten or fifteen minutes.

COCOA.

Two tablespoonfuls of cocoa-nibs.
Half a pint of boiling water.
Half a pint of boiling milk.
One teaspoonful of sugar.

Boil the nibs in the water one hour, and strain.

Add the milk, and boil ten minutes longer. Sweeten, and serve hot, with toast.

Time required, one hour and a quarter.

BROMA.

Two tablespoonfuls of broma.
Six tablespoonfuls of boiling water.
One pint of boiling milk.
One teaspoonful of sugar.

Blend the broma with the boiling water, pour it into the boiling milk, stirring all the while, and simmer until it thickens.

Sweeten, and serve hot, with dry toast.

Time required, ten or twelve minutes.

WATERS.

BRAN WATER.

Two quarts of good wheat bran.
Three quarts of cold water.

Put the bran into a large bowl, stir the water into it, and let it soak over night.

Then rub and squeeze the bran with the hands until all the flour which adheres to it is washed off:

strain through a fine sieve, pressing and squeezing until the bran seems quite dry.

N. B.—The white, starchy-looking water thus procured contains the cerealin and vegetable casein, both of which are necessary elements of nutrition.

BARLEY WATER.

Half a pint of pearl barley.
Two quarts of boiling water.
One saltspoonful of salt.

Wash the barley thoroughly, put it into a double kettle or saucepan with the boiling water, and simmer three hours.

Strain, and add the salt.

Two tablespoonfuls of cream and one teaspoonful of sugar make it much more palatable.

One teaspoonful of lemon juice may be used instead of the cream, if desired.

Time required, three hours.

ALMOND BARLEY WATER.

One-fourth of a pint of blanched almonds.*
Half a pint of pearl barley, well washed.
Three pints of boiling water.
Two teaspoonfuls of sugar.

* See Blanched Almonds.

Pound the almonds in a mortar until quite fine, and put them into a saucepan with the barley, water, and sugar.

Boil all together until the water is about the consistency of cream.

Strain, and serve either hot or cold.

Time required, two hours.

EGG WATER.

The whites of two eggs.
Half a pint of cold water.
Sugar or salt.

Blend the eggs with the water, by stirring gently (not beating), and add half a *tea*spoonful of sugar or half a *salt*spoonful of salt, to make it palatable.

Time required, about five minutes.

N. B.—This is highly recommended by physicians for children with diarrhœa, while teething.

OATMEAL WATER NO. 1.

Two large tablespoonfuls of fine oatmeal.
One pint of boiling water.
Half a teaspoonful of sugar.
Half a saltspoonful of salt.

Pour the boiling water over the oatmeal, stir it well, and strain through a fine wire sieve.

Add the sugar and salt, and drink either hot or cold.
Time required, ten minutes.

OATMEAL WATER NO. 2.

Two tablespoonfuls of fine oatmeal.
One pint of cold water.

Stir the oatmeal into the water, and let it stand one hour; then strain it through a fine sieve, and drink cold.

Time required, about one hour.
N. B.—An excellent drink in hot weather.

RICE WATER.

Four tablespoonfuls of rice.
One quart of cold water.
One quart of boiling water.

Wash the rice thoroughly, put it into a saucepan or double kettle with the cold water, and place it on the back part of the stove (where it will keep hot but not boil), and let it remain one hour.

Add the boiling water, and simmer slowly until the rice is nearly all dissolved.

Strain, and drink either hot or cold.
Time required, about two hours.

TAPIOCA WATER.

One tablespoonful of tapioca.
One-fourth of a pint of cold water.
One pint of boiling water.

Wash the tapioca well, and soak it in the cold water two hours.

Pour the boiling water over it, and boil slowly until the tapioca is dissolved.

Time required, three hours.

N. B.—Good in cases of nausea.

TOAST WATER.

Three slices of stale bread.
One quart of boiling water.

Toast the bread slowly in the oven to a very dark brown; put it into a pitcher, and pour the boiling water over it.

Cover close, and let it stand until cold; strain and serve ice-cold.

Time required, about one hour.

N. B.— Good in cases of nausea and thirst arising from diarrhœa.

BURNT TOAST WATER.

Three slices of stale bread.
One quart of boiling water.

Toast the bread in the oven until it is burnt and

looks very black; put it into a pitcher with the boiling water, cover close and let stand until cold.

Strain when required for use.

Time required, about an hour.

MINT WATER.

One-fourth of a pint of green spear-mint leaves.

Half a pint of boiling water.

Bruise the mint leaves, put them into a bowl and pour the boiling water over them; cover close and let it steep ten minutes.

Strain, and drink either hot or cold.

Time required for steeping, ten minutes.

N. B.—This is a very acceptable drink in cases of nausea.

GUM ARABIC WATER.

Two teaspoonfuls of gum arabic.

One teaspoonful of sugar.

One pint of hot water.

Place all the ingredients in a small pitcher, and leave it on the stove where it will keep hot, until the gum is dissolved.

Serve cold.

Time required, about two hours.

N. B.—Lemon juice may be added to this if desired.

TAMARIND WATER.

One tablespoonful of tamarinds.
Half a pint of ice water.
One teaspoonful of sugar.

Put the tamarinds into the water, and stir until they are as nearly dissolved as they can be.

Strain into a goblet, and add the sugar.

Time required, about ten minutes.

N. B.—A cooling, delicious, and wholesome drink.

PEACH WATER.

One pint of dried peaches.
One quart of boiling water.

Pick over and wash the peaches until perfectly clean; put them into a pitcher, pour the boiling water over, and cover closely until cold.

Strain as required for use.

Time required, two hours.

N. B. If stimulant is required, brandy or wine may be added to the water.

APPLE WATER NO. 1.

Five large, juicy, tart apples, unpared.
One quart of boiling water.
One teaspoonful of sugar.

Slice the apples into a pitcher, and pour the boiling water over them.

Cover close until cold, then strain and sweeten.
Time required, about an hour and a half.
N. B.—A cooling and slightly laxative drink.

APPLE WATER NO. 2.

One pint of dried apples.
One quart of boiling water.

Pick over and wash the apples until perfectly clean; put them into a pitcher, pour the boiling water over, and cover closely until cold.

Strain as required for use.

Time required, two hours.

JELLY WATER.

Two tablespoonfuls of boiling water.
Two tablespoonfuls of any acid fruit jelly.
Half a pint of ice water.

Put the boiling water and jelly into a goblet, stir until the jelly is dissolved, then add the ice water.

Time required, about five minutes.

HOT JELLY WATER.

Two tablespoonfuls of any acid fruit jelly.
Half a pint of boiling water.

Put the jelly into a goblet, pour the boiling water over it, and stir until the jelly is dissolved.

Time required, about ten minutes.
N. B.—If taken very hot, will induce perspiration.

WHEYS.

RENNET WHEY.

One quart of fresh milk, slightly warmed.
Half a saltspoonful of salt.
One tablespoonful of "rennet wine." *

Pour the milk into a shallow dish; add the salt and wine, stirring only enough to mix it.

When cold and stiff, cut it across a number of times to free the whey.

Strain through a fine sieve or a thin piece of muslin.
Time required, about half an hour.
N. B.—A tablespoonful of rich cream added to the whey will render it more palatable and nutritious.

WINE WHEY.

One pint of new milk.
One-fourth of a pint of any acid wine.
One teaspoonful of sugar.

Heat the milk to the boiling point, and pour the wine into it.

Simmer *very gently* until the whey separates from the curd.

* See Rennet Wine.

Strain and sweeten.
Time required, about ten minutes.

TAMARIND WHEY.

Two tablespoonfuls of tamarinds.
One pint of new milk, boiling hot.
One teaspoonful of sugar.

Put the tamarinds into the boiling milk, and simmer until the whey appears.

Strain and sweeten.
Time required, about ten minutes.

LEMON WHEY.

One tablespoonful of lemon juice.
One pint of new milk, boiling hot.
One teaspoonful of sugar.

Stir the lemon juice into the boiling milk, and simmer *very gently* until the whey appears.

Strain and sweeten.
Time required, about ten minutes.

VINEGAR WHEY.

One tablespoonful of pure vinegar.
One pint of new milk, boiling hot.
One teaspoonful of sugar.

Stir the vinegar into the milk, and simmer gently until the whey appears.

Strain and sweeten.

Time required, about ten minutes.

LEMONADES.

LEMONADE, NO. 1.

Two tablespoonfuls of lemon juice.
One tablespoonful of sugar.
Half a pint of ice water.
One tablespoonful of pounded ice.
Two thin slices of lemon.

Put all the ingredients into a large goblet, and stir until the sugar is dissolved.

Time required, about five minutes.

LEMONADE NO. 2.

Two tablespoonfuls of lemon juice.
One tablespoonful of sugar.
Half a pint of boiling water.

Put all the ingredients into a hot bowl, and stir until the sugar is dissolved.

Drink it hot.

Time required, about ten minutes.

EGG LEMONADE.

One egg, well beaten.
Two tablespoonfuls of sugar.
The juice of half a large lemon.
Two tablespoonfuls of cold water.
One pint of pounded ice or ice raspings.

Beat the egg and sugar together until very light, and stir in the lemon juice and water.

When well blended, add the ice, and drink through a straw.

Time required, about ten minutes.

FLAX SEED LEMONADE.

Three tablespoonfuls of flax seed.
Two tablespoonfuls of sugar.
One pint of boiling water.
Three tablespoonfuls of lemon juice.

Put the flax seed and sugar into a pitcher, pour the boiling water over them, and steep on the back part of the stove one hour.

Strain, add lemon juice, and serve cold.

Time required, about an hour.

IRISH MOSS LEMONADE.

One-fourth of a pint of Irish moss.
One quart of boiling water.
Six tablespoonfuls of lemon juice.
Four tablespoonfuls of sugar.

Wash the moss thoroughly, and let it soak in cold water ten minutes; then remove all imperfect parts and any gravel that may adhere to it.

Put it into a pitcher with all the other ingredients, cover closely, and steep on the back part of the stove two hours.

Strain through a wire sieve, and drink either hot or cold.

Time required, about two hours and a half.

MISCELLANEOUS.

CURRANT SHRUB.

One-fourth of a pint of cold water.
Five tablespoonfuls of red-currant juice.
Two tablespoonfuls of ice raspings.
One tablespoonful of sugar.

Put the above ingredients into a tumbler, and stir until the sugar is dissolved.

A very refreshing and palatable drink.

Time required, about ten minutes.

HORSFORD'S ACID PHOSPHATE.

One teaspoonful of Horsford's acid phosphate.
Half a pint of water.
One tablespoonful of sugar.
Three tablespoonfuls of pounded ice.

Put all the ingredients into a pitcher, and stir until the sugar is dissolved.
Time required, about five minutes.
N. B.—This is an excellent drink in cases of nervous fevers, and is much like lemonade in taste.

MINT JULEP.

Five tablespoonfuls of ice water.
Four tablespoonfuls of pounded ice.
One tablespoonful of sugar.
Two tablespoonfuls of brandy or whisky.
A handful of bruised mint leaves.

Place all the ingredients in a goblet, and stir until the sugar is dissolved.
Stick a few sprigs of mint in for ornament.
Drink through a straw.
Time required, about ten minutes.

TODDY.

Half a teaspoonful of sugar.
Six teaspoonfuls of water, either hot or cold.
Four teaspoonfuls of brandy or whisky.

Dissolve the sugar in the water, and stir in the brandy or whisky.
Time required, two or three minutes.

GROG.

One tablespoonful of brandy or whisky.
Three tablespoonfuls of cold water.

RENNET WINE.

One calf's rennet.
One quart of sherry wine.

Cut the rennet into pieces about an inch square, and put them into a bottle with the wine; cork tight, and set it away in a cool place. In two days it will be ready for use.

One tablespoonful will coagulate one quart of milk.
Time required, twenty-four hours.

SHERRY CLARET, OR CATAWBA COBBLER.

Four tablespoonfuls of wine.
Four tablespoonfuls of cold water.
One scant tablespoonful of sugar.
Six tablespoonfuls of pounded ice.

Place all the ingredients in a large tumbler, and stir until the sugar is dissolved.
Drink through a straw.
Time required, about ten minutes.

PORTEREE.

One-fourth of a pint of cold water.
Four tablespoonfuls of porter or brown stout.
One teaspoonful of sugar.
Four tablespoonfuls of pounded ice.

Place all the ingredients in a large goblet, and stir until the sugar is dissolved.
Grate a little nutmeg over the top, if desired.
Drink through a straw.
Time required, about ten minutes.

SYLLABUB.

Two teaspoonfuls of sugar.
One tablespoonful of wine.
One pint of new milk.

Dissolve the sugar in the wine, and put it into a pint pitcher.
Take it to the cow and milk into it, until the foam reaches the top.
Time required, about ten minutes.

TOAST WINE.

One slice of well browned toast.
Half a pint of boiling water.
One teaspoonful of sugar.
Two tablespoonfuls of wine.

Put the toast into a pitcher, pour the boiling water over, and let it stand until cold.

Then strain off the water, and to it add the sugar and wine.

Time required, about an hour.

ORGEAT.

One-fourth of a pint of sweet almonds, blanched.*
One teaspoonful of orange-flower water.
One pint of new milk.
One pint of water.
Two scant teaspoonfuls of sugar.

Pound the almonds in a mortar until they are well broken.

Moisten with the orange-flower water and rub them to a smooth paste.

Pour in the milk and water, a little at a time, stirring all the while, that the ingredients may be well blended.

Strain and sweeten.

Time required, about one hour.

---

* TO BLANCH ALMONDS.—Pour boiling water over the almond meats, and let them stand a few minutes to loosen the skin; then wipe them as dry as possible and slip the skins off.

SAGO MILK.

One tablespoonful of pearl sago.
Four tablespoonfuls of cold water.
One quart of new milk.

Wash the sago well, and soak it in the water over night.

Put it into a double kettle with the milk, and boil until the sago is clear and almost dissolved.

Sweeten, and drink either hot or cold.

Time required (after soaking), one hour.

MULLED WINE.

Two teaspoonfuls of broken cinnamon.
Six whole cloves.
One-fourth of a pint of boiling water.
Two eggs.
Two tablespoonfuls of sugar.
Half a pint of wine, boiling hot.

Steep the spices in the boiling water ten minutes, and strain.

Beat the eggs and sugar together until *very light*, and stir it into the spiced water.

Add the hot wine, and allow the whole to simmer until it *begins* to thicken, stirring slowly all the while.

Pour it from one pitcher to another three or four times, to make it foamy and light.

Serve it either hot or cold.

Time required, about twenty minutes.

MULLED CIDER.

One pint of cider (a little acid, but not hard).
One teaspoonful of whole cloves.
Three eggs, well beaten.
One tablespoonful of sugar.

Boil the cider and cloves, together three minutes.

Put the eggs and sugar into a pitcher, beat until very light, and pour the boiling cider into it, stirring rapidly to prevent curdling.

Pour the mixture from one pitcher to another until it is foamy and light.

Serve hot in glasses, with a very little nutmeg grated over the top.

Time required, about fifteen minutes.

KOUMISS NO. 1.

One even tablespoonful of sugar.
A piece of compressed yeast the size of a hazelnut.
Two tablespoonfuls of warm water.
One quart of fresh milk, slightly warmed.

Dissolve the sugar and yeast in the warm water, and put it into a strong two-quart bottle with the milk; do no fill the neck of the bottle.

Cork tight, wire, and keep in a warm place (about as warm as required to raise bread) twenty-four hours, or until it begins to look thick; then put it where it will be kept *very cold* until required for use.

Shake well, and draw from the bottle through a wine faucet.
Time required, five or six days.

KOUMISS NO. 2.
One pint and a half of new milk.
Half a pint of warm water.
One tablespoonful of home-made yeast.
One even tablespoonful of sugar.

Place all the ingredients in a strong quart bottle, but do not fill the neck.

Cork tight, wire, and keep in a warm place (about as warm as required to raise bread) twenty-four hours, or until it begins to look thick; then put it where it will keep *very cold* until needed.

Shake well, and draw from the bottle through a wine faucet.
Time required, five or six days.

PUNCHES.

RUM PUNCH.
One teaspoonful of sugar.
Half a pint of new milk.
Two tablespoonfuls of rum.

Dissolve the sugar in the milk, stir in the rum, and mix well by pouring from one glass to another, twice.
Time required, about two minutes.

ROMAN PUNCH.

One pint of cold water.
One-fourth of a pint of granulated sugar.
One-fourth of a pint of orange juice.
Six tablespoonfuls of lemon juice.
Six tablespoonfuls of pure Jamaica rum.
One-fourth of a pint of Champagne.
One-fourth of a pint of powdered sugar.
The stiff-beaten whites of four eggs.

Put the first six ingredients into a freezer, packed in ice; stir until the sugar is dissolved, and freeze the whole until it begins to thicken.

Then whip the powdered sugar and beaten eggs together until very light, stir it into the punch, and freeze until stiff.

Time required, about one hour.

MILK PUNCH.

Half a pint of fresh milk, ice-cold.
Two teaspoonfuls of sugar.
Four tablespoonfuls of brandy.

Put the milk into a goblet with the sugar and brandy, and stir until the sugar is dissolved.

Time required, three or four minutes.

N. B.—In cases of bowel trouble, use boiling milk instead of cold.

EGG AND MILK PUNCH.

One egg, well beaten.
One tablespoonful of sugar.
Half a pint of sweet milk, ice-cold.
Four tablespoonfuls of brandy or whisky.

Beat the egg and sugar together until very light, and stir it into the milk.
When well mixed, add the brandy or whisky.
Time required, five or six minutes.

SHERRY PUNCH.

One-fourth of a pint of rich milk.
One teaspoonful of sugar.
Two tablespoonfuls of sherry wine.

Put the milk into a goblet, dissolve the sugar in it, and add the wine.
Time required, about five minutes.

EGG-NOGGS.

EGG-NOGG.

Two eggs.
Two tablespoonfuls of powdered sugar.
Half a pint of new milk.
Half a pint of sweet cream.
Six tablespoonfuls of brandy or whisky.

Beat the yolks of the eggs and sugar together until very light.

Stir in the milk and cream, and when well blended with the egg, add the brandy or whisky.

Lastly, whip in the whites of the eggs, which have been beaten to a stiff froth.

Serve in small goblets, with a grate of nutmeg over the top of each.

Time required, about fifteen minutes.

HOT EGG-NOGG.

The yolk of one egg.
One scant tablespoonful of sugar.
One pint of boiling milk.
Two tablespoonfuls of brandy or whisky.

Beat the egg and sugar together until quite light, and stir it briskly into the boiling milk.

Add the brandy or whisky, and serve in a goblet, with a very little nutmeg grated over the top.

Time required, about fifteen minutes.

SUMMER EGG-NOGG.

One egg.
One tablespoonful of powdered sugar.
Half a pint of cream.
One-fourth of a pint of ice raspings.
Four tablespoonfuls of brandy or wine.

Beat the yolk of the egg and sugar together until very light.

Stir in the cream and ice raspings, and when well blended with the egg, add the brandy or wine.

Lastly, whip in the white of the egg, which has been beaten to a stiff froth.

Serve in small goblets, with a very little nutmeg grated over the top of each.

Time required, about ten minutes.

EGG AND WINE NO. 1.

One egg.
Four tablespoonfuls of cold water.
Four tablespoonfuls of wine.
One teaspoonful of sugar.
Nutmeg, if desired.

Beat the egg (yolk and white together) until very light, and stir the cold water into it.

Heat the wine, dissolve the sugar in it, and pour it into a saucepan with the egg.

Simmer *slowly* until it *begins* to *thicken*, stirring one way all the time.

When done, pour it into a tumbler, and grate a little nutmeg over the top.

Serve immediately.

Time required, about fifteen minutes.

EGG AND WINE NO. 2.

One egg.
Two teaspoonfuls of sugar.
Four tablespoonfuls of cold water.
Four tablespoonfuls of sherry wine.

Beat the egg and sugar together until very light; pour in the water, and stir until well blended.

Add the wine, and serve immediately.

Time required, about ten minutes.

EGG AND BRANDY.

The whites of two eggs.
Two teaspoonfuls of powdered sugar.
Two teaspoonfuls of brandy or rum.

Beat the eggs to a stiff froth, whip in the sugar, and lightly stir in the brandy or rum.

Time required, about ten minutes.

N. B.—Very delicious when frozen.

EGG FLIP.

One egg.
Four teaspoonfuls of sugar.
Half a pint of hot beer, not boiling.

Beat the egg and sugar together until *stiff* and *light.*

Pour the hot beer into it, stirring briskly to prevent curdling, and pour it from one bowl to another to make it foamy and light.

Time required, about ten minutes.

N. B.—This is used when stimulant and nourishment are required, and should only be taken in small quantities, unless otherwise ordered by the physician.

FLUMMERIES.

BRAN FLUMMERY.

One pint of bran water.*
Two teaspoonfuls of corn starch or wheat flour.
Two tablespoonfuls of cold water.
One saltspoonful of salt.

Put the bran water in a saucepan or double kettle and stir gently until it begins to simmer.

Blend the flour or corn starch with the cold water, and stir it into the boiling bran water.

Add the salt, and cook until the flummery looks clear.
Serve hot, with cream and a little sugar.

Time required, about thirty minutes.

OATMEAL FLUMMERY NO. 1.

One pint of "Hornby's Steam Cooked Oats."
Two quarts of cold water.
One teaspoonful of salt.

* See Bran water.

Put the oats into a bowl, stir the water into it, and let it soak one hour.

Then rub and squeeze with the hands until all the flour which adheres to the grain is washed off.

Strain through a fine sieve, pressing and squeezing until the oats seem quite dry.

Put the starchy-looking water thus obtained into a double kettle, add the salt, and cook until the flummery looks clear, stirring occasionally to prevent lumps.

Serve with cream and sugar.

Time required, about an hour and a half.

N. B.—If in haste, the *soaking* may be omitted. Flummery made from this preparation of oats is *entirely* free from the *bitter* taste which is so objectionable in the common oatmeal.

OATMEAL FLUMMERY NO. 2.

One quart of medium oatmeal.
One quart of tepid water.
One quart of boiling water.
One teaspoonful of salt.

Put the oatmeal into a large bowl, pour two gallons of cold water over it, stir well, and let it stand over night.

In the morning drain off the water as long as it looks clear; add to the meal two gallons of fresh water, stir well, and strain it through a wire sieve into a broad pan.

This should be kept in a cool place forty-eight hours, changing the water night and morning.

When the last water has been drained off, blend the tepid water with the starch that is in the bottom of the pan; pour it into the boiling water (which should be in a double kettle), stirring briskly to prevent lumps. Add the salt, and cook until the flummery looks clear.

Serve either hot or cold, with cream and sugar.

Time required after soaking, about three-quarters of an hour.

N. B.—This is the Scotch and Irish mode of preparing flummery. The process seems a tedious one, but, if strictly adhered to, will amply repay you for the trouble. It is wholesome and nutritious for both invalids and children.

CUSTARDS.

RENNET CUSTARD.

One egg.
One teaspoonful of sugar.
Half a pint of new milk.
One teaspoonful of rennet wine.

Beat the egg and sugar together until stiff and light.

Heat the milk to about the same temperature as

when drawn from the cow, and stir it into the egg and sugar.

Pour it into a bowl (the one in which it is to be served), and add the wine, stirring only enough to mix.

Set it in a cool place. It will stiffen in a few minutes, and be ready for use as soon as cold.

Time required, about half an hour.

N. B.—This is a delicious custard, and is more digestible than one that is cooked. It is very much like a baked custard.

BAKED CUSTARD.

Three dessertspoonfuls of sugar.

One quart of new milk.

Three eggs, well beaten (yolks and whites together).

Half a saltspoonful of cinnamon.

Dissolve the sugar in the milk, and stir in the eggs and cinnamon.

Pour it into an earthen pudding dish, and bake in a moderate oven until the custard "sets," and is a light brown on the top.

Remove it immediately from the oven, otherwise the whey will appear, and the custard is spoiled.

Time required for cooking, about twenty minutes.

BOILED CUSTARD.

One quart of new milk.
Three eggs, well beaten (yolks and whites together).
Three dessertspoonfuls of sugar.
One teaspoonful of corn starch.
The stiff-beaten whites of two eggs.

Put the milk into a double kettle, and heat it to the boiling point.

Beat the *three* eggs, sugar and corn starch well together, and pour the mixture slowly into the boiling milk, stirring gently to prevent sticking.

When almost boiling, and about the consistency of thick cream, remove from the fire and pour it into a bowl to cool.

When cold, stir in the beaten whites of the two eggs, and serve very cold.

Time required, about an hour.

SAGO CUSTARD NO. 1.

One-fourth of a pint of fine pearl sago.
Half a pint of cold water.
Half a pint of boiling water.
One and a half pints of boiling milk.
Two eggs.
Two dessertspoonfuls of sugar.
Eight drops of vanilla essence or two teaspoonfuls of brandy.

After the sago has been thoroughly washed and drained, soak it in the cold water over night.

Pour the boiling water over it, and simmer until perfectly clear; then add the boiling milk, and when it is well blended with the sago, remove from the fire.

Beat the yolks of the eggs with the sugar until quite light, and stir it into the sago; when about *half* cold, add the vanilla or brandy.

When *cold*, whip in the whites of the eggs, which have been beaten to a stiff froth.

Serve cold, in custard cups or glasses.

Time required after soaking, about one hour.

SAGO CUSTARD NO. 2.

One-fourth of a pint of fine pearl sago.
Half a pint of cold water.
Half a pint of boiling water.
Half a pint of boiling milk.
Two eggs.
Three dessertspoonfuls of sugar.
Nutmeg.

After the sago has been thoroughly washed and drained, soak it in the cold water over night.

Pour the boiling water over it, and simmer until it looks clear.

Add the boiling milk, and when it is well blended with the sago, remove it from the fire.

Stir in the eggs, which have been beaten with the

sugar until very light; flavor slightly with nutmeg, and bake in a quick oven twenty minutes.

Serve (either hot or cold) with cream and sugar if desired.

Time required after soaking, about forty minutes.

RICE CAUDLE.

One-fourth of a pint of Carolina rice.
Three pints of boiling water.
Half a saltspoonful of salt.
The yolk of one egg.
One tablespoonful of sugar.
Four tablespoonfuls of sherry wine.

Pick over and wash the rice, put it into a double kettle with the water and salt, and boil slowly one hour.

Strain off the water, and bring it to a boil.

Beat the egg and sugar together until very light, and stir it slowly into the boiling rice water.

Add the wine, and serve immediately.

Time required, about an hour and a quarter.

EGG CAUDLE.

Three whole cloves.
Half a teaspoonful of broken cinnamon.
Half a pint of boiling water.
One egg.
One teaspoonful of sugar.
One teaspoonful of brandy.

Steep the spices in the boiling water ten minutes, and strain.

Beat the egg and sugar together until very light, and pour the spiced water onto it, stirring briskly until well blended.

Simmer until it *begins* to thicken, then add the brandy, and pour the caudle from one glass to another two or three times, to make it foamy and light.

Serve either hot or cold.

Time required, about fifteen minutes.

N. B.—This is very nice without the brandy, which, if not desired, can be left out.

ORANGE CAUDLE.

One tablespoonful of Cox's gelatine.

Two tablespoonfuls of hot water.

One pint of new milk, boiling hot.

One teaspoonful of sugar.

Two tablespoonfuls of orange juice.

Dissolve the gelatine in the hot water, and pour it into the boiling milk.

Simmer slowly two or three minutes, and remove from the fire.

Add the sugar, and, when about half cold, stir in the orange juice, which will make it about the consistency of thick cream.

Serve immediately.

Time required, from a half to three-quarters of an hour.

RENNET CURD.

One quart of fresh milk.
One tablespoonful of rennet wine.
Half a saltspoonful of salt.

Warm the milk to about the same temperature as when drawn from the cow, and add the wine, stirring only enough to mix it.

When cold and stiff, cut across a number of times, and strain through a piece of thin muslin.

When the curd is quite free from whey, put it into a bowl, add the salt, and stir until it is creamy and light.

Serve with cream, and a little sugar if desired.

Time required, about three-quarters of an hour.

BLANC-MANGES.

RENNET BLANC-MANGE OR JUNKET.

One quart of new milk, slightly warmed.
One tablespoonful of sugar.
One tablespoonful of rennet wine. *

While the milk is warming, dissolve the sugar in it.

When it is about the temperature of milk just drawn from the cow, pour it into a bowl (the one in which it is to be served), and stir in the wine.

* See Rennet Wine.

This stiffens in a few minutes, and is ready for use as soon as cold.

Serve with or without cream.

Time required, about half an hour.

IRISH MOSS BLANC-MANGE.

One-fourth of a pint of Irish moss, well washed.
One quart of new milk, boiling hot.
Four teaspoonfuls of sugar.
Six drops of essence of vanilla, or any flavor desired.

Soak the moss in a little cold water five minutes; take it out of the water, put it into the boiling milk, and simmer until it is about the consistency of cream.

Sweeten, flavor, and strain through a wire sieve into a mould to cool.

When cold, turn it out of the mould into a dish, and serve with cream and sugar.

Time required, three-quarters of an hour.

ARROWROOT BLANC-MANGE.

Four tablespoonfuls of Bermuda arrowroot.
One-fourth of a pint of cold milk.
One pint of boiling milk.
Two teaspoonfuls of sugar.
One-fourth of a saltspoonful of salt.
A grate of nutmeg or ten drops of brandy.

Blend the arrowroot with the cold milk, and pour

it slowly into the boiling milk (which should be in a double kettle), stirring all the time.

Add the sugar and salt, and cook fifteen minutes.

Flavor and pour it into a mould to cool.

When cold, turn it into a dish, and serve with cream and sugar.

Time required, one hour.

RICE-CREAM BLANC-MANGE.

Three tablespoonfuls of Carolina rice.
Four tablespoonfuls of thick, sweet cream.
Four tablespoonfuls of Madeira wine.
One teaspoonful of sugar.

Pick over and wash the rice well, put it into a double kettle, and boil, with as much milk as it will absorb, until it is thoroughly done.

Pulp it through a fine wire sieve, and set it aside to cool.

When cold, add the cream, and whisk it to a froth, then stir in the wine and sugar.

Serve very cold.

Time required, one hour and a half.

FARINA BLANC-MANGE.

One pint of boiling milk.
One pint of boiling water.
Four tablespoonfuls of farina.
One saltspoonful of salt.

Heat the milk and water in a double kettle, and, when boiling, sprinkle in the farina, stirring all the time to prevent lumps.

Boil slowly twenty minutes; add the salt, stir well, and turn it into a mould to cool.

Serve with cream and sugar, and, if allowed, a grate of nutmeg over it.

Time required, about an hour.

CORN-STARCH BLANC-MANGE.

Two heaping tablespoonfuls of corn starch.
Four tablespoonfuls of cold milk.
One pint of boiling milk.
Two teaspoonfuls of sugar.
Half a saltspoonful of salt.

Blend the starch with the cold milk, and pour it slowly into the boiling milk (which should be in a double kettle), stirring all the time to prevent lumps.

Add the sugar and salt, and cook fifteen minutes; flavor if desired, and pour it into a mould to cool.

When cold, turn it out of the mould into a dish, and serve with cream and sugar, or stewed fruit.

Time required, about an hour and a half.

PUDDINGS.

BREAD PUDDING.

Half a pint of dry, toasted crust crumbs.
One pint of boiling milk.
One egg.
One tablespoonful of sugar.
A grate of nutmeg.

Grate the crumbs into a small pudding dish, pour the boiling milk over them, cover close, and set aside to cool.

Beat the egg and sugar together until very light, and stir it into the bread and milk, which should be nearly cold.

Flavor, and bake in a brisk oven.

Serve hot, with wine-sauce or cream.

Time required for baking, twenty minutes.

RICE PUDDING.

One quart of cold milk.
One-fourth of a pint of rice, well washed.
One-fourth of a pint of sugar.
Half a teaspoonful of salt.
One quart of boiling milk.
Nutmeg.

Put the cold milk into a pudding dish with the rice, sugar and salt, and bake in a *slow* oven.

Stir the top under every half hour, and each time add half a pint of the boiling milk.

Flavor delicately with nutmeg, and serve either hot or cold, with cream.

Time required, about two hours and a half.

STEAMED RICE.

Half a pint of Carolina rice.
One pint of fresh milk.
Half a teaspoonful of salt.

Pick over and wash the rice, put it in a two-quart dish with the milk and salt, and set it in a steamer with a tight-fitting cover. Steam two hours, stirring lightly with a fork now and then to keep the grains from packing.

Serve with cream and sugar.

Time required, two hours.

BROWNED RICE.

Half a pint of well browned rice.
Three-fourths of a pint of cold water.
Half a teaspoonful of salt.

Put the above ingredients into a two-quart dish, set it in a steamer with a close cover, and steam an hour and a half.

Serve with cream and sugar.

Time required after the rice is browned, about an hour.

JELLIES.

CHICKEN JELLY.

One chicken, weighing two and a half or three pounds.
Three pints of cold water.
One teaspoonful of salt.
A light shake of black pepper.

After the chicken has been thoroughly cleaned, and soaked an hour in cold water, put it into a kettle with the three pints of water, and salt, and boil slowly until the meat drops from the bones and the water is reduced to one pint.

Add the pepper, and strain the broth through a piece of thin muslin into a mould, to cool and harden.

When cold and firm, remove the fat, and serve the jelly in thin slices, with bread or crackers.

Time required, three or four hours.

SAGO WINE JELLY.

One tablespoonful of pearl sago.
Half a pint of cold water.
One tablespoonful of sugar.
Two tablespoonfuls of sherry wine.

Wash the sago well, and soak it in the cold water over night.

Put it, with the same water, into a saucepan over a slow fire, and simmer until perfectly clear.

Add the sugar and wine, and when cold, serve with cream, and more sugar if desired.

Time required after soaking, about an hour.

ARROWROOT WINE JELLY.

Two tablespoonfuls of Bermuda arrowroot.
Four tablespoonfuls of cold water.
Half a pint of boiling water.
Two teaspoonfuls of sugar.
Two tablespoonfuls of wine or brandy.

Blend the arrowroot well with the cold water, and strain it through a double piece of bobbinet into the boiling water, stirring briskly all the time.

Add the sugar, and simmer five minutes, or until it looks perfectly clear; remove from the fire, and stir in the brandy or wine.

When cold, serve with cream, and more sugar if desired.

Time required, ten or fifteen minutes.

TAPIOCA LEMON JELLY.

One tablespoonful of tapioca.
Three-fourths of a pint of cold water.
Five teaspoonfuls of sugar.
Two teaspoonfuls of lemon juice.

Wash the tapioca thoroughly, soak it in the cold water over night, then simmer slowly until perfectly clear and smooth.

Stir in the sugar and lemon juice, and turn it into a dish. Serve either hot or cold, with cream.

Time required after soaking, about fifteen minutes.

BARLEY JELLY.

Two tablespoonfuls of " Robinson's Patent Barley." *
Four tablespoonfuls of cold water.
Half a pint of boiling water.
Two teaspoonfuls of sugar.
Half a saltspoonful of salt.
A grate of nutmeg, or any flavoring preferred.

Stir the barley flour and cold water together until well blended, pour it into the boiling water and simmer half an hour, stirring gently all the while.

Add the sugar, salt and flavoring, and serve either hot or cold, with cream.

Time required, about forty minutes.

CORN-STARCH WINE JELLY.

Two tablespoonfuls of corn starch.
Four tablespoonfuls of cold water.
Two teaspoonfuls of sugar.
Half a pint of boiling water.
Two tablespoonfuls of sherry wine.

* Kept by druggists.

Blend the starch with the cold water.

Dissolve the sugar in the boiling water, and pour the starch into it, stirring briskly all the time.

Simmer until it looks clear; add the wine, and turn it into a dish.

Serve either hot or cold, with cream.

Time required, if used hot, fifteen minutes.

TOAST JELLY.

Four slices of stale bread.
One quart of boiling water.
Four tablespoonfuls of sugar
A grate of nutmeg.

Toast the bread slowly to a rich brown; put it into a saucepan with the boiling water and sugar, and simmer until the whole becomes a glutinous mass.

Remove it from the fire, and rub through a wire sieve; flavor, and turn it into a dish to cool and harden.

Serve with cream.

Time required, about an hour and a half.

ISINGLASS WINE JELLY.

Half an ounce (a sheet and a half) of Cooper's isinglass.
One pint of hot water (not boiling).
Four tablespoonfuls of sugar.
One-fourth of a pint of sherry wine.

Dissolve the isinglass in the hot water, add the sugar, and heat the whole to the boiling point (do not boil).

Remove from the fire, stir in the wine, and let it stand one minute.

Strain it through a flannel jelly-bag into a mould, and set it in a cold place to cool and harden.

Time required, three or four hours.

N. B.—If the jelly is required in haste, strain it into a shallow dish; it will harden much quicker in that way

CALF'S FOOT JELLY.

One set of calf's feet, thoroughly cleaned, but not skinned.

One gallon of cold water.

One pint of granulated sugar.

One pint of sherry wine.

The juice of two lemons and thinly pared rind of one.

The stiff-beaten whites and crushed shells of six eggs.

Split the calf's feet, put them into a kettle with the cold water, bring slowly to a boil, and skim.

Simmer slowly six hours, or until the water is reduced to about three pints, and strain it through a fine sieve into a dish to cool.

When cold and firm, remove all fat and dregs.

Put the jelly and sugar into a porcelain kettle, and stir until the sugar is dissolved; then add the wine, lemon and egg; stir well, and boil briskly two minutes.

Take it off the fire, let it stand two minutes, then remove the scum.

Strain through a flannel jelly-bag into a mould, and set it on ice to harden.

Time required, about twelve hours.

JELLY WITH ICE.

One-fourth of a pint of pounded ice.
Half a pint of wine jelly.
Two tablespoonfuls of sherry wine.

Stir the ice and jelly together, put it into a glass bowl, and pour the sherry over it.

Time required, about five minutes.

GELATINE WINE JELLY.

Half a box (or three-fourths of an ounce) of Cox's gelatine.
Half a pint of cold water.
Half a pint of boiling water.
Half a pint of sugar.
Half a pint of sherry wine.
Half a lemon — juice and thinly pared rind.
The stiff-beaten white and crushed shell of one egg.
A grate of nutmeg.
A small stick of cinnamon.

Soak the gelatine in the cold water one hour, pour it into a saucepan with the boiling water and sugar, and stir until both gelatine and sugar are dissolved.

Then add the wine, lemon, egg, nutmeg, and cinnamon, and boil briskly half a minute.

Remove from the fire, and let it stand half a minute, then skim, and strain through a flannel jelly-bag into a mould. The mould should be wet in cold water before straining the jelly into it.

Place it on ice to harden.

If required in haste, use a shallow dish instead of a mould to cool it in.

Time required, five or six hours.

JELLIED WINE.

One tablespoonful of gelatine.
Two tablespoonfuls of cold water.
Two tablespoonfuls of sugar.
One-fourth of a pint of wine.

Dissolve the gelatine in the water by slowly heating it, stirring at the same time.

Dissolve the sugar in the wine, pour it into the gelatine, and stir until they are well blended.

Turn it into a tumbler, and set it on ice to cool and harden.

Time required, about three hours.

N. B.—Wine can sometimes be taken in this way

when the patient cannot *drink* it. No boiling is required.

CREAMS.

TAPIOCA CREAM.

Two-thirds of a pint of tapioca.
Half a pint of cold water
One quart of new milk.
Two eggs.
Four tablespoonfuls of powdered sugar.
Four drops of any essence preferred.

After the tapioca has been well washed, soak it in the cold water seven or eight hours, or until it is tender.

Put it into a double kettle with the milk, and cook until dissolved and well blended with the milk.

Beat the *yolks* of the eggs and the sugar together until very light, stir it into the tapioca, and remove at once from the fire.

When nearly cold, stir in the *whites* of the eggs, which have been beaten to a stiff froth.

Flavor and serve cold.

Time required after soaking, two hours.

WHITE BAVARIAN CREAM.

Half a box of Cox's gelatine.
Five tablespoonfuls of cold water.
One pint of fresh milk.
One-fourth of a pint of sweet cream.
Two tablespoonfuls of granulated sugar.
The stiff-beaten whites of four eggs.
Two tablespoonfuls of powdered sugar.
One tablespoonful of brandy.

Soak the gelatine in the cold water one hour, or until it is dissolved.

Heat the milk and cream to the boiling point, add the granulated sugar, and stir until it is dissolved.

Strain the gelatine through a piece of fine net into the milk, stir well, and set it aside to cool and harden.

Beat the eggs to a *stiff, dry froth*, and whip in the powdered sugar and brandy.

When the gelatine mixture is quite cold, and has begun to harden, stir it until it is perfectly smooth, then as lightly as possible whip the eggs into it.

Turn the whole into a glass dish, and set it in the refrigerator to stiffen, which will take two hours.

Serve *very cold*.

Time required, about three hours and a half.

N. B.—If this cream is desired soft like a custard, use one-third of a box of gelatine instead of half a box.

GOLDEN BAVARIAN CREAM.

Half a box of Cox's gelatine.
Five tablespoonfuls of cold water.
One pint of fresh milk.
One-fourth of a pint of sweet cream.
Two tablespoonfuls of granulated sugar.
The stiff-beaten whites of four eggs.
Two tablespoonfuls of powdered sugar.
Eight drops of any essence preferred.
The yolks of two eggs.

Soak the gelatine in the cold water one hour, or until it is dissolved.

Heat the milk to the boiling point, add the granulated sugar and stir until it is dissolved.

Strain the gelatine through a piece of fine net into the milk, stir well, and set it aside to cool and stiffen.

Beat the whites of the eggs to a *stiff, dry froth*, and whip in the powdered sugar and flavoring. When the gelatine mixture is quite cold, and has begun to harden, beat it until it is perfectly smooth, then stir in the yolks of the two eggs which have been beaten until very light. Lastly, whip in the whites of the eggs.

Turn the whole into a glass dish, and set it in the refrigerator to cool and harden, which will take two hours.

Time required, about three hours and a half.

ICE CREAM.

One tablespoonful of Bermuda arrowroot.
Four tablespoonfuls of cold milk.
Half a pint of sugar.
One quart of boiling milk.
One pint of rich cream.
Six drops of any flavoring preferred.

Blend the arrowroot with the cold milk, and strain it through a double piece of bobbinet.

Dissolve the sugar in the boiling milk (which should be in a double kettle), and pour the arrowroot into it, stirring gently to prevent lumps.

Simmer until it thickens, and turn it into a dish to cool.

When cold, stir in the cream and flavoring. Freeze.

Time required, about two hours.

ICE CREAM.

One pint of thick, sweet cream.
Two tablespoonfuls of powdered sugar.

Whip the cream to a stiff froth, stir in the sugar, a little at a time, and flavor if desired.

Put it into a freezer, packed in ice and salt, just as you would for other ice cream; do not stir it, but let it stand until frozen.

If the weather is cold enough, it will freeze by leaving it out-of-doors.

Time required, about one hour.

N. B.—This is very rich, and should only be taken in small quantities.

CAKES.

WHITE SPONGE CAKE.

One teaspoonful of cream of tartar.
Three-fourths of a pint of sifted flour.
One-third of a saltspoonful of salt.
The whites of eleven eggs.
One even pint of *granulated* sugar.
Six drops of essence of almond or vanilla.

Put the cream of tartar into the flour and sift it (through a *fine* sieve) *six* times.

Sprinkle the salt over the eggs, and beat them to a *stiff* froth.

Stir the sugar into the beaten eggs as lightly as possible, and then add the flour in the same manner; lastly the flavoring.

The *mixing* must be done very quickly with a spoon-shaped wire egg-beater.

Turn the batter immediately into a round, three-quart pan with a tube in the center; do not grease or paper the pan.

Bake in a moderate oven fifty-five minutes.

Stick a broom-straw into it, and if it comes out clean, the cake is done.

Turn the pan upside down, and let it rest on the tube one hour.

When entirely cool, it will loosen itself from the pan, and can be easily removed with the aid of a sharp knife.

Time required, about an hour.

PLAIN SPONGE CAKE.

One-third of a saltspoonful of salt.
Six eggs, very fresh.
Three-fourths of a pint of powdered sugar.
Six drops of essence of lemon.
One even pint of thrice-sifted flour.

Sprinkle the salt over the whites of the eggs, and beat them to a *very* stiff froth.

Beat the yolks of the eggs ten minutes; add the sugar and essence, and beat five minutes longer.

Stir the white into the yellow as lightly as possible, and then add the flour in the same manner.

The mixing must be done very quickly, with a spoon-shaped wire egg-beater.

Turn the batter immediately into a round three-quart pan; do not grease or paper the pan.

Bake in a moderate oven fifty minutes.

Stick a broom-straw into the cake, and if it comes out clean, the cake is done.

Turn the pan upside down, and let it rest on the tube one hour.

When entirely cool, it will loosen itself from the pan, and can be easily removed with the aid of a sharp knife.

Time required, nearly an hour.

ADDITIONAL RECIPES.

EGG BROTH.

One egg, well beaten.
Half a teaspoonful of white sugar.
One pint of boiling water.
Half a saltspoonful of salt.

Beat the egg and sugar together until very light, and pour the boiling water into it, stirring briskly to prevent curdling.

Add the salt, and serve it hot.

Time required, five or six minutes.

N. B.—This broth requires very little effort of the stomach to digest it, and is highly recommended in cases of extreme exhaustion.

MILK AND WATER.

Half a pint of fresh milk.
Half a pint of boiling water.

The milk and water should be mixed and taken hot.

This drink is absorbed into the system in a very few minutes after it is taken into the stomach, and is recommended by physicians in cases of exhaustion, especially after hemorrhage or fainting.

RAW BEEF SANDWICH.

A small saltspoonful of salt.
One-third of a saltspoonful of pepper.
Two tablespoonfuls of scraped beef.
One slice of slightly buttered bread.

Rub the salt and pepper into the meat, and spread it on the bread; fold and cut it into three strips.

RUSK.

Toast dry crusts of bread in a moderate oven until they are brown (not burnt) through and through.

When cold, pound them in a mortar until reduced to a coarse meal, then sift it through a flour sieve into a dish.

Serve with milk or cream, and sugar if desired.
Time required, about six hours.

FOOD FOR INFANTS.

MILK FOOD.

Half a pint of freshly made whey.*
Two tablespoonfuls of fresh cream.
Half a teaspoonful of sugar of milk.

Warm the whey to about the normal temperature of the body, add the cream and sugar, and stir until the sugar is dissolved.

Time required, about three-quarters of an hour.

N. B.—This food is especially suitable for infants from one to six months old, and can be conveniently taken from a feeding-bottle.

BARLEY FOOD.

One teaspoonful of "Robinson's Patent Barley." †
Three teaspoonfuls of cold water.
One-fourth of a pint of boiling water.
Half a saltspoonful of salt.
One-fourth of a pint of fresh milk.
Half a teaspoonful of sugar of milk.

Stir the barley flour and cold water to a smooth paste, and pour it into the boiling water; add the salt, and simmer twenty-five minutes.

Then pour it into the milk, add the sugar, and serve immediately.

* See Rennet Whey.   † Kept by Druggists.

FOOD FOR INFANTS.

Time required, about half an hour.

N. B.—This is excellent for young children, particularly if they are inclined to constipation.

BRAN FOOD.

Half a pint of bran water.*
One-fourth of a pint of fresh milk.
One tablespoonful of cream.
One teaspoonful of sugar of milk.

Boil the bran water slowly for twenty minutes, then add the milk, cream, and sugar; let it cool to about the normal temperature of the body, and serve immediately.

This is especially good for young children.

OATMEAL FOOD.

One-fourth of a pint of "Hornby's Steam Cooked Oats."
One pint of cold water.
Two tablespoonfuls of fresh cream.
One teaspoonful of sugar or sugar of milk.
One saltspoonful of salt

Soak the oats in the water one hour, then rub it well with the hands, and strain through a double piece of fine net.

* See Bran Water.

Boil slowly about half an hour, add the cream, sugar, and salt, and serve it warm.

Time required, about an hour and a half.

N. B.—If in haste, the soaking may be omitted. This is very palatable, and does well for young children, particularly if inclined to constipation.

ARROWROOT FOOD.

One teaspoonful of Bermuda arrowroot.
Three teaspoonfuls of cold water.
One-fourth of a pint of boiling water.
Half a saltspoonful of salt.
One-fourth of a pint of fresh milk.
Half a teaspoonful of sugar of milk.

Stir the arrowroot and cold water to a smooth paste, and strain it through a piece of fine net into the boiling water; add the salt, and simmer thirty minutes. Then pour it into the milk, add the sugar, and give it to the child warm.

N. B.—This can be given from a feeding-bottle.

ALMOND MILK.

One-fourth of a pint of blanched *sweet* almonds.*
One pint of boiling water.
One teaspoonful of sugar of milk.

Pound the almonds in a mortar until reduced to

---

* See Blanched Almonds.

a smooth paste; add the boiling water to it, stir well, and strain through a piece of fine muslin.

Sweeten and serve warm.

Time required, about an hour.

This milk will sometimes agree with infants, when they cannot take cow's milk.

BOILED FLOUR.

One pint of wheat flour.
Four tablespoonfuls of cold water.

Moisten the flour with the water, press it into a ball, and tie it tight in a strong cloth; dampen the cloth, dredge with flour, put it into boiling water, and let it boil hard ten hours.

Remove the cloth and let the ball dry in a moderate oven or in the hot sun.

Time required, about twenty-four hours.

BOILED FLOUR PAP.

One teaspoonful of boiled flour.
Two tablespoonfuls of cold water.
One-fourth of a pint of boiling milk.
One-third of a teaspoonful of sugar of milk.

Grate the flour from the ball, blend it with the water to a smooth paste, and stir it into the boiling milk.

Simmer about three minutes and add the sugar.

Time required after the flour is boiled, about ten minutes.

N. B.—This pap is considered good for children, with diarrhœa, while teething.

NUTRITIVE ENEMATA.

Nutritive aliments are sometimes required for rectal use; where there is difficulty in introducing food into the stomach, or where the character of the disease requires absolute rest of the digestive organs, life can be sustained in this manner for an indefinite period.

The rectum and colon are comparatively deficient in the fluids that are necessary for the digestion of the alimentary material; therefore the food must be artificially digested, or brought in contact with such substances as will prepare them for rapid absorption.

The large intestine has few lacteals compared with the small intestine, yet it is undeniably a fact that absorption takes place, and the food serves quite as good a purpose for some time, when introduced through the rectum as when taken through the natural channel.

The material to be injected should be tepid, and given very slowly, so that the intestine will not contract and expel the fluid. This direction is important,

NUTRITIVE ENEMATA.

as the rectum will not tolerate sudden distention, but is very tolerant of fluid administered cautiously.

If stimulants are needed, they may be given in cream, or milk made richer by the addition of cream.

While milk or whey are the substances most frequently used, quite a bill of fare can be prepared; for when rectal feeding is continued for some time, *variety* of food is needed as in stomachical diet.

The following articles in addition to milk and whey are suitable for injections:

Beef tea, beef broth, or similar preparations of mutton and chicken.

Raw beef tea, beef blood, or the compounds of these with whey or milk.

Raw eggs mixed with water, broth or milk.

Cod liver and other oils.

If the mixed diet set up fermentation in the intestine, as exhibited by foul excretion of flatus or fæces, inject burnt toast water* occasionally.

Thirst may be quenched by the use of a small quantity of water given per rectum, once or twice daily.

As all rectal enemata will be given under the direction of the physician in charge of the patient, he will determine the especial food required for the individual case, and also the quantity to be administered in the twenty-four hours.

For the artificial digestion of rectal foods, pepsin and pancreatine are the two important substances to

---

* See Burnt Toast Water.

be used. Pepsin for all animal foods, and pancreatine if there is any fat or oily matter to be digested.

Add from three to eight grains of pepsin to half a pint of broth, let it stand in a warm place twenty minutes, then strain through a fine net, and inject.

For the preparation of whey, use the formula for rennet whey.

For Beef Tea, Raw Beef Tea, Beef Broth, and Burnt Toast Water, see Index.

N. B.—*All enemata should be warmed to the normal temperature of the body.*

SUGGESTIONS FOR THE SICK-ROOM.

In the following practical suggestions, I do not claim anything new or original; they are only a few of the items that we learn by experience to be essential to the comfortable condition of the sick.

Few persons think much of the value of such knowledge, until the necessity for action presses upon them; and then, through fear and anxiety, are wholly unfitted to assume the responsibility and care.

To the inexperienced, therefore, I hope this may be a help in their hour of need.

The sick-room should be kept scrupulously neat and orderly, and thoroughly ventilated by allowing a continuous supply of fresh air from the outside, and a free escape of *foul* air, regulating the temperature of the apartment by a thermometer—which should be kept at from 68° to 70°, unless otherwise ordered by the physician. An open fire-place is the best promoter of ventilation. A fire should be kept burning in it,—even in summer, a slight fire of kindlings night and morning.

Let the light and sunshine freely into the room, being careful to shield the *eyes* from the glare. The habit of placing sick persons in close, dark rooms, is pernicious both to body and mind. The cheerful, purifying effect of the sun's rays is of inestimable value to the well-being and speedy recovery of the sick.

Always endeavor to inspire the patient with confidence in your capacity and desire to do anything that might add to his comfort; it should be the special aim of the attendant to relieve him of all care and anxiety about himself, and as far as possible his mind should be kept calm and hopeful.

Speak gently, and in quiet, subdued tones; a loud voice grates harshly on sensitive nerves.

Do not whisper; it causes great anxiety to the patient to feel that his ailments are being discussed in inaudible tones. He is often suspicious, his imagination is vivid, and the presumption to him becomes a reality of wonderful proportions. A low, well modulated voice will seldom disturb the most sensitive patient.

It is well to note down the physician's directions in regard to giving medicines, etc., as the fatigue and anxiety incident to sickness renders the memory unreliable.

Use a glass spoon for giving medicine, and never, under any circumstance, give it in the dark.

When it is difficult for a patient to drink from a tumbler, a bent glass tube will be found convenient.

Have the patient rinse the mouth frequently with

SUGGESTIONS FOR THE SICK-ROOM.

water, to which a little vinegar, aromatic ammonia, or lemon juice, has been added; or, if too weak to do so, the attendant can take strips of old linen and use as swabs. This should not be neglected, especially in the morning and before eating.

Bathe the entire body often; if done under cover, with water to which a little alcohol or ammonia has been added, there need be no fear of taking cold.

In contagious diseases, put four drops of pure carbolic acid to a quart of water, and sponge with it.

Another refreshing wash —

One cupful of water.
One cupful of alcohol.
One tablespoonful of salt.
One ounce of aromatic ammonia. Bottle and keep it ready for use.

When the patient is uneasy and restless, pour some into the hand, and rub the body with it until a pleasant glow is felt; it is refreshing, and very beneficial as a tonic.

This is highly recommended by the writer's physician.

In cases of severe illness, keep visitors out of the room; or, if admitted at all, they should never enter into discussions of any kind; their conversation should be cheerful, and stay short, avoiding all unpleasant subjects, bad news, or anything of an exciting nature.

Especially should they be excluded after five o'clock

in the afternoon; their presence interferes with the routine duties of the nurse, fatigues the already weary patient, who, unconscious of the cause, becomes nervous and restless; and the result is often the loss of sleep which otherwise might have been obtained.

Extra care should be taken not to disturb the sleep or rest of a sick person.

Always remember the sick-room should be *kept quiet*.

Much suffering would be avoided if thoughtless friends would heed these admonitions.

When making up a bed for a patient that is feeble and unable to help himself, take two sheets and fold them twice, lengthwise; lay them across the bed — one under the hips, the other under the shoulders; by taking firm hold of the ends of the sheets on one side of the bed, and gently drawing toward you, it will be easy to move the patient from one side to the other. To *turn* the patient, slightly lift the sheets as you draw them.

A little practice will soon enable the attendant to change the position of the patient with ease and comfort.

If possible, change the bed linen daily, and air the blankets and other bedding as often, but not in the room with the patient.

Avoid drafts of air on the patient, and do not let him sit up long enough to become wearied. An *extra* bed in the room, to which he can be moved daily, will be a grateful and salutary change, and will allow time to make up and air the bed.

It is a great convenience, and almost a necessity, to have two or three small pillows to place under the knees and other parts of the body, as rests or props to relieve the strain upon the enfeebled muscles.

Do not sit or lie down on the bed; for no matter how quiet you may be, it is thoughtless to subject a sick person to anything that may annoy.

Chloride of lime is a good disinfectant and great purifier. One pound of chloride of lime requires three gallons of water. Put the solution in earthen vessels and place them in different parts of the room.

A solution of carbolic acid can be used in the same manner, or saturate cloths with it and pin them to articles of furniture in the room.

Phenol sodique, as a disinfectant, is prompt and reliable, and highly recommended by physicians. It can be procured at any drug-store, with labeled instructions for use.

Dissolve copperas, and put a small quantity in the vessels used, to prevent unpleasant odors.

A stool-chair for the convenience of the patient is a positive necessity, and all matters discharged should be removed immediately, in the same vessel, from the room.

To wring flannels out of hot water, fold the cloths the desired size; place them in the center of a small towel, and dip it in the hot water, keeping the ends of the towel dry to handle. By using the towel as a wringer, the cloths will be much hotter than if wrung with the naked hands.

An India-rubber bag for hot water is a great convenience in the room, as it is easily removed to any part of the body.

A pair of long, soft, wool stockings should be kept handy to draw on when the feet and limbs are cold.

To preserve ice, take a piece of flannel eighteen inches square, cut a small hole in the center, and place it over a wide-mouthed pitcher; sink it half way down, and secure it around the pitcher with a string; fill it up with small pieces of ice, cover well with a double thickness of flannel; the water will drip from the flannel into the pitcher, leaving the ice dry.

If these instructions are observed, small pieces of ice can be kept many hours.

Too much attention cannot be given to the proper preparation of food, and the most dainty manner of presenting it to an invalid.

It often taxes, to the fullest extent, our efforts in his behalf, and requires the most delicate suggestions of taste and beauty to tempt the capricious appetite.

The careful, tasteful arrangement of the tray, with snowy napery and choice china, served by a cheerful attendant, will greatly add to the enjoyment of the meal. Always remember to serve *freshly prepared food*, and in small quantities.

Do not feel discouraged if your efforts to please the appetite are unavailing, or not appreciated; it is one of the common incidents of the sick-room, and must be philosophically accepted.

Do not consult with a patient as to what he would like to eat; appropriate food should be given without his care. When a meal is finished, remove all articles of diet from the room, and do not leave delicacies intended for his use within sight.

Never allow a patient to become faint or exhausted for want of nourishment.

In convalescence, food should be given in great moderation. "Little and often" is a safe rule.

www.ingramcontent.com/pod-product-compliance
Lightning Source LLC
Chambersburg PA
CBHW020125170426
43199CB00009B/636